Contents

The Recording

Ukulele and Vocals: Fred Sokolow
Recorded at Sossity Sound by Michael Monagan

To access audio visit:
www.halleonard.com/mylibrary

Enter Code
7396-0838-1430-1375

T0057660

7777 W. BLUEMOUND RD. P.O. BOX 13819 MILWAUKEE, WI 53213

Publisher: Jim Beloff
Edited by Ronny S. Schiff
Cover and Art Direction by Elizabeth Maihock Beloff
Graphics and Music Typography by Charylu Roberts
Fred Sokolow photo by Lynn Shipley Sokolow

Introduction

You may have noticed that jazz players seldom play the same chords you play when you read from a songbook. Through the miracle of jazz wizardry, they enhance simple chord progressions and make them more interesting, prettier, subtler…*jazzier*.

This book demystifies that wizardry for uke players. You'll learn the principles of *jazz chord substitution* that allow you to jazz up any tunes that need that something extra. You'll become a more advanced strummer, and beyond that, you'll have a better understanding of how chord progressions work, and how to vary them. You may be able to play a song hundreds of times and never play it the same way twice!

Here's how it works:

- First, you'll learn to strum the chords to an old standard like "Back Home In Indiana," with the basic chords found in most songbooks.

- Then you'll learn a fancier accompaniment, enhanced by chord substitutions.

- Next, you'll learn the reasons for every change from the original chord progression. Each variation, chord-by-chord, is explained according to a principle of *chord substitution*.

- Finally, you'll learn a chord/melody arrangement for the tune (in which you play chords and melody at the same time), using the enhanced, jazzed-up chords.

After going through this process with several tunes, you'll start to assimilate the substitution ideas, enabling you to jazz up any tunes you like, both in backup and chord/melody playing.

The audio that comes with this book includes all the arrangements, as written, so you can compare each tune's basic chord backup to the jazzed-up version, and you can hear the timing that's so crucial for translating tablature into music. Dive in, and take your strumming, chord chops, and your understanding of music in general, to the next level!

Enjoy!

Fred Sokolow

www.sokolowmusic.com

Visit us on the web at **www.fleamarketmusic.com**

How To Use This Book

To get the most out of the pages that follow, read the next chapter on "Some Basic Music Theory." Then, for each song…

- Listen to the "Basic Backup and Melody" track several times and strum along with it until the tune is familiar.

- Read the "About the Progression" text that describes how the chord progression works.

- Listen to the "Backup with Substitutions" track several times and play along with it. If the track is too fast for you, play the arrangement slower, by yourself (without the recording).

- Read the "How the Substitutions Work" text that explains why the altered or additional chord changes work.

- ***Every time a new substitution idea comes up, it will be in boldface, so you'll know it's an important concept to grasp!***

- To learn the chord/melody solos, listen to the recorded track, then practice playing it on your own. Once you're familiar with it, play along with the recording. Notice that the chord solo of each tune resembles the "Backup with Substitutions" arrangement, but some changes have been made to include or highlight the melody.

- There's an Index at the back of the book that lists all the substitution ideas alphabetically, and tells the song and bar in which each one first appeared. Whenever a substitution is explained (e.g., "Dm7 is a *dominant minor substitution* for G7"), you can go to the Index to refresh your memory regarding that principle.

Some Basic Music Theory

To many people, music theory is confusing and intimidating. You could ignore this chapter and you'd probably learn some chord substitution ideas by osmosis, if you just play the simple versions of the songs in this book, and compare them to the "jazzed up" versions. But if you understand the basics of music theory and how chord progressions work, you'll get so much more out of the pages ahead.

So, it's time to tackle a few basic concepts of music theory and wrestle them to the ground. For starters, what does it mean to say a song is in the key of C?

Keys

A key is a tonal home base. If a song is in the key of C, it feels at rest when the C chord is played. Moving to any other chord causes tension, and the tension is resolved when you go back to the C chord. Try strumming this progression (four strums on each chord), and stop on any chord other than C; you'll feel that unresolved tension. Stop on the C chord and you'll hear/feel the *resolution*:

Dm | G7 | C | Am |

A song's ending chord is almost always the *tonic* — the chord that names your key (like a C chord, in the key of C).

The Numbers System

The language of music is often expressed with numbers rather than letters. Musicians talk about 2-5-1s and 6-2-5-1s. They say, "Go to the 4 chord," or "Go to the 2 minor." The numbers refer to the major scale. For example, the C major scale is: C, D, E, F, G, A, B, C. Since C is the first note in the C major scale, a C chord is the 1 chord in the key of C. D, or D7 or Dm is the 2 chord; E is the 3 chord, and so on. In the key of D, E is the 2 chord.

No matter which key you're in, going from the 1 chord to the 5 chord has a certain sound. So does going from 1 to 4. It's the spaces between chords (the chord intervals, e.g., the distance between a 1 chord and a 4 chord) that give a song its unique chord progression. Once you can recognize the sounds of the various intervals (1 to 4, 2– to 5)*, you understand how music works, and you can play a song in any key. You're not just memorizing letter names; you're feeling the song's structure.

The 1-4-5 Chord Family

Regardless of a song's key, the 1, 4 and 5 chords are the "usual suspects" — the chords that are most likely to occur. Millions of songs in the folk, country, blues, bluegrass and classic rock genre consist of just those three chords. They can be in any order imaginable. It's helpful to have the chord families memorized: 1, 4 and 5 in the key of C = C, F and G, for example.

---

* In the numbers system, "two minor" is written "2–."

Relative Minors

Every major chord has a *relative minor*, a closely related chord that is a sixth higher. For example, D is the sixth note in the F major scale, so Dm is the relative minor of F. If you play an F chord and a Dm chord on the uke (the easy, first-position chords), you'll see how similar they are. If you strum the F and the Dm over and over in a rhythm, you'll recognize the familiar *sound* of the relative minor in context.

If a tune has more than just the immediate chord family (1, 4 and 5), the next chords most likely to occur are the relative minors of 1, 4 or 5. In the key of C, for example, C, F and G are the immediate chord family, and their relative minors, Am, Dm and Em make an extended chord family. A song in the key of C is likely to include any one, two or all three of these minor chords.

The Circle-Of-Fifths

This chart groups chords in their 1-4-5 chord families. For example, if you look at the C at the top of the chart, the note F (or chord) that's a fourth above C is one step clockwise. The note G (or chord) a fifth above C is one step counter-clockwise.

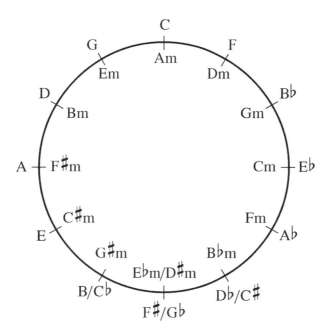

The same applies in any key. The chart says that if you're in the key of E, the 4 chord is A (one step clockwise) and the 5 chord is B (one step counter-clockwise).

The chords inside the circle are relative minors, so the chart enables you to view any extended chord family at a glance. For example, looking at the key of G: C (one step clockwise) is the 4 chord, and Am is its relative minor; D (one step counter-clockwise) is the 5 chord, and its relative minor is Bm; and G is the 1 chord, and Em is its relative minor.

The circle chart is also useful because many chord progressions consist of (or include) circle-of-fifths motion. That means you leave the chord family and return to the 1 chord by going up by 4ths. This happens, for example, in these typical first eight bars of "Five Foot Two, Eyes of Blue," "Please Don't Talk About Me When I'm Gone" and many other songs:

C | E7 | A7 | A7 | D7 | G7 | C | C |

The key here is C. You leave the C chord family when you go to E7. Then you go up a fourth to A7 (A is the fourth note in the E major scale), up a fourth to D7 (D is a fourth above A) and up another fourth to G7 (G is a fourth above D) and up still another fourth to C, finally resolving the progression (coming back to the home base).

As you ascend by fourths, the chords along the way can be minors instead of sevenths. One of the most often-used circle-of-fifths progressions is the "Rhythm Changes," named after Gershwin's "I Got Rhythm." It's 1, 6-, 2-, 5, or, in the key of C:

C Am | Dm G7 |

Countless pop songs include the "Rhythm Changes." Some examples: "Blue Moon," "Be My Baby," "Heart And Soul," "Please Mr. Postman" and "Stand By Me." Sometimes the entire song is 1, 6-, 2-, 5, over and over again, as in "Stand By Me."

Some songs consist entirely of circle-of-fifths chord movement, and in other tunes part of the song goes up by fourths and the rest makes use of the immediate chord family or some other harmonic device, such as…

Diatonic Progressions

In many songs, the chords go up or down the major scale of the song's key. For instance, if the song is in the key of C, the chords may be: C, Dm, Em, F, G, which is 1, 2-, 3-, 4, 5. That's how "Like A Rolling Stone" begins. Another part of the song descends: F, Em, Dm, C (4, 3-, 2-, 1). "Here, There And Everywhere" and "Lean On Me" both contain the ascending chords: 1, 2-, 3-, 4, and "Lean On Me" comes back down: 4, 3-, 2-, 1.

In all three songs, the 2 and 3 are minor and the other chords are major. That's because the chords in songs like this are usually *diatonic*, or "of the major scale." In diatonic progressions, all the chords are built from the notes in the major scale of the song's key. If a diatonic song is in C, all its chords are built from notes in the C major scale. This results in the following chords:

1	2	3	4	5	6	7
C (1)	Dm (2-)	Em (3-)	F (4)	G (5)	Am (6-)	Bdim (7°)
		or C/E (1/3)		or C/G (1/5)	or F/A (4/6)	or Bm7♭5 (7-7♭5)
					or Dm/A (2-/6)	or G/B (5/7)
						or Em/B (3-/7)

As the above chart shows, there are options for some of the intervals. For example, the seventh chord can be diminished (Bdim, in the key of C) or it can be a minor seven, flat five chord (Bm7♭5).

The fraction chords in the above chart, like C/E, are inversions: chords with a bottom note that is not the root of the chord (such as a C chord with an E note in the bass). *Since the most common uke tuning includes a high-G 4th string, you have no bass string.* So, you can ignore the right-hand side of the inversions, and play a C chord where C/E is indicated.

Jazz players often play diatonic progressions instead of playing a single chord for two bars, to create a feeling of movement. Given two bars of C, you can play: C Dm | C/E Dm |

Sometimes, diminished chords are played between the 1 and 2 minor or the 2 minor and 1/3. For example: C, C♯dim, Dm, D♯dim, C/E.

Chord Types

The three most-often-used types of chords are majors, minors and sevenths. (There are also diminished and augmented chords, but they'll be discussed later.) Major chords are built on the 1st, 3rd and 5th intervals. For example, a C major chord consists of C, E and G, the 1st, 3rd and 5th notes in the C major scale:

- Minor chords are built on the 1st, ♭3rd and 5th intervals (Cm = C, E♭ and G).

- Seventh chords are built on the 1st, 3rd, 5th and ♭7th intervals (C7 = C, E, G, B♭).

- There are variations of each chord type. For example:

  - C becomes C6 when you add a 6th, or Cmaj7 when you add a 7th.

  - Cm becomes Cm7 when you add a flatted 7th, or Cm6 when you add a 6th.

  - C7 becomes C9 when you add a 9th (which is the same as a 2nd). It becomes C7sus when you raise the 3rd a half step to a 4th.

All the variations add color, but as long as you stay within the chord type, you're okay. For instance, if you're reading a songbook and it calls for Cm6, you can get away with a Cm. Instead of C9, you can play a C7. It will still sound correct; it'll just be a bit less subtle.

Chords With Multiple Names

Some chord shapes can have two or even three names. For example, this shape:
can be called C6 or Am7, because those two chords consist of the same four
notes: C, E, G and A. Which name you use is arbitrary, but it's helpful to name a chord according to its context in a progression. Throughout this book you may see a chord grid and find its letter-name puzzling ("Am7? My uke chord book says that's a C6!"). It's one of those multi-named chord shapes. Here are some more examples:

Am7♭5 or Cm6   Bb9 or Fm6   Adim or B7♭9

These music theory concepts will make it easier to understand the explanations of *substitutions* in the arrangements that follow.

Prologue

The four substitution ideas used in "Red River Valley," below, are used in *all* the tunes that follow, so it's crucial that you understand them before moving on!

Before diving head first into the jazz tunes, get your feet wet with a simple, three-chord folk tune (just to give you an idea of how chord substitution works). There are twenty-four substitution ideas in this book, but you'll deal with four of them here:

Four Substitution Concepts

- **Direct substitution:** *You can substitute any chord from the same chord type as the given chord.* For example, for C7 you could play C9, C7+ or C13, just to name a few, because all these chords are C7 with an extra note added (a 9th, a sharp 5th, etc.). They're variants of a C7 chord.

- **Relative minor substitution:** *For a major chord, you can often substitute or add the relative minor.* That's the minor chord that's a 6th above the major chord. For example, A is the sixth note in the C major scale, so Am is the relative minor of C. Given a C chord, you can play Am, or a C followed by an Am.

- **Dominant minor substitution:** *Given a 7th chord, you can add or substitute the minor chord that is a 5th above it.* For example, given a C7 you can substitute Gm (a 5th above C7), or play Gm followed by C7.

- **Ascending or descending melodic lines:** *A series of chords can contain an ascending or descending melodic line that harmonizes with the song's melody.* You'll find a few examples in the sample tune below. The effect is like ear candy—two melodies happening simultaneously that harmonize with each other.

Now, you can put these four concepts to use in the old cowboy song, "Red River Valley." First, listen to the basic tune as written below, and then play along with the recording using simple, first-position chords:

RED RIVER VALLEY

TRACK 1

        C   G7   C   G7
Come and sit by my side if you love me. Do not hasten to bid me adieu.

        C   C7   F   G7   C
But remember the Red River Valley, and the cowboy who loved you so true.

Here's a jazzed-up version. Listen to the recording and play along with it:

RED RIVER VALLEY
With Substitutions

TRACK 2

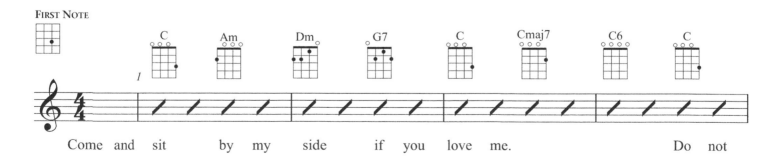

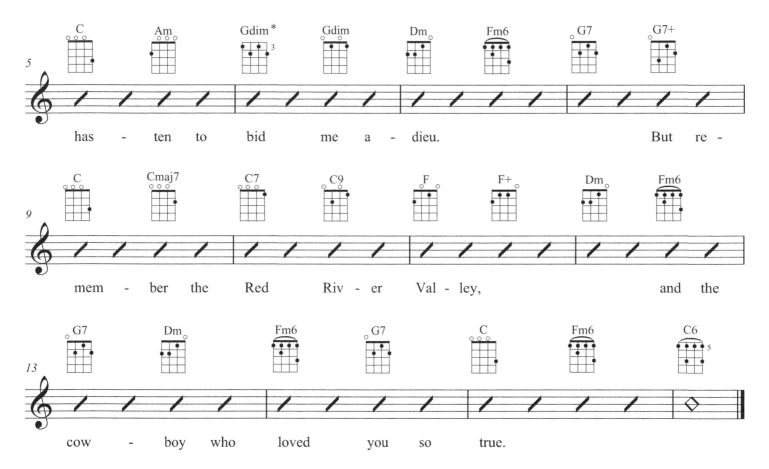

The first bar is a "pickup bar," and the song actually starts at the bar numbered as "1" ("sit by my…"). Now if you compare the basic progression to the fancier comping (backup) chords, most of the differences between the two can be explained in terms of the four substitution concepts above.

Bar 1: Am is a *relative minor substitution* for C.

Bar 2: Dm is a *dominant minor substitution* for G7, as Dm is a fifth above G.

Bars 3–4: Cmaj7 and C6 are *direct substitutions* for C. The series of chords (C, Cmaj7, C6, C) contain a *descending melodic line:* C, B, A, G.

Bar 5: Am is a *relative minor substitution* for C.

Bar 7: Dm is a *dominant minor substitution* for G7.

Bar 8: G7+ (G augmented, or a G chord with a sharp fifth) is a *direct substitution* for G.

Bars 9–10: Cmaj7 is a *direct substitution* for C, and C9 is a *direct substitution* for C7. The series of chords (C, Cmaj7, C7) contain a *descending melodic line:* C, B, B♭, similar to the melodic line in bars 3–4.

Bars 11–12: F+ is a *direct substitution* for F, and Dm is a *relative minor substitution* for F.

Bar 13: Dm is a *dominant minor substitution* for G7.

Bar 16: C6 is a *direct substitution* for C.

I know, I know, some things are unexplained! What about the G diminished chords in bar 6, or the Fm6 chords (there are four of them)? Remember, there are twenty more substitution principles that haven't been described yet. Read on, and expand your chord consciousness!

---

* The "3" next to the Gdim grid indicates that this chord is played on the 3rd fret.

BACK HOME IN INDIANA
Basic Backup and Melody

BACK HOME IN INDIANA
About the Progression

This Tin Pan Alley tune was written in 1917 and has long been a standard amongst Dixieland and jazz players. For years, it was Louis Armstrong's opener at performances, and Miles Davis based the bebop instrumental, "Donna Lee," on the chord progression. Since 1946, it has been played at the Indianapolis 500 races. At one point, "Indiana" briefly quotes the lyrics and melody of a much older song, "On The Banks Of The Wabash."

Play along with the recording and strum the chords to "Indiana." Then read the following notes about the chord progression. It'll be helpful to recognize some basic facts about the structure of the tune, before altering or jazzing up the chords.

The Basic Progression

Because songs like "Indiana" have been recorded by so many artists and bands, for so many decades, you'll find many variations of the chord progression in songbooks, sheet music and online "tab" sites. In its oldest, simplest form, here it is in numbers, and in letters, in the key of F:

1 | 6^7 | 2^7 | 2^7 | 5^7 | 5^7 | 1 | 1^7 | 4 | $1°$ | 1 | 1 | 2^7 | 2^7 | 5^7 | 5^7 |

1 | 6^7 | 2^7 | 2^7 | 5^7 | 3^7 | 6- | 4- | 1 | 3^7 | 6- | 2^7 | 1 | 5^7 | 1 | 1 ‖

F | D7 | G7 | G7 | C7 | C7 | F | F7 | B♭ | Fdim | F | F | G7 | G7 | C7 | C7 |

F | D7 | G7 | G7 | C7 | A7 | Dm | B♭m | F | A7 | Dm | G7 | F | C7 | F | F ‖

This is a 32-bar tune, the standard number of bars for countless pop tunes. The last 16 bars begin as a repeat of the first 16; then they go off in a different direction…also typical of Tin Pan Alley tunes. Notice that the song has plenty of circle-of-fifths movement, including several 6–2–5–1s, some 2–5–1s and some near 3–6–2–5–1s that get sidetracked or skip a chord. For example, D7–G7–C7–F is a 6–2–5–1 in the key of F, and G7–C7–F is a 2–5–1. Halfway through the first sixteen bars, the F diminished chord takes you from B♭ back to F. This chord movement (4–1dim–1) happens in many songs.

Pickup Bars: The "Basic Backup and Melody" chart on the previous page starts with a bar of lyrics with no chord, instead of the 1 chord shown above. It's a "pickup bar," a sort of intro that occurs in many songs. If a bandleader counted to four to start the tune (as they often do), they'd go "One, two, three, four, one." After the second "one" you'd start singing "Back home again, etc." and you'd begin strumming the 1 chord at the "-gain" of "again," as heard on the recording.

BACK HOME IN INDIANA

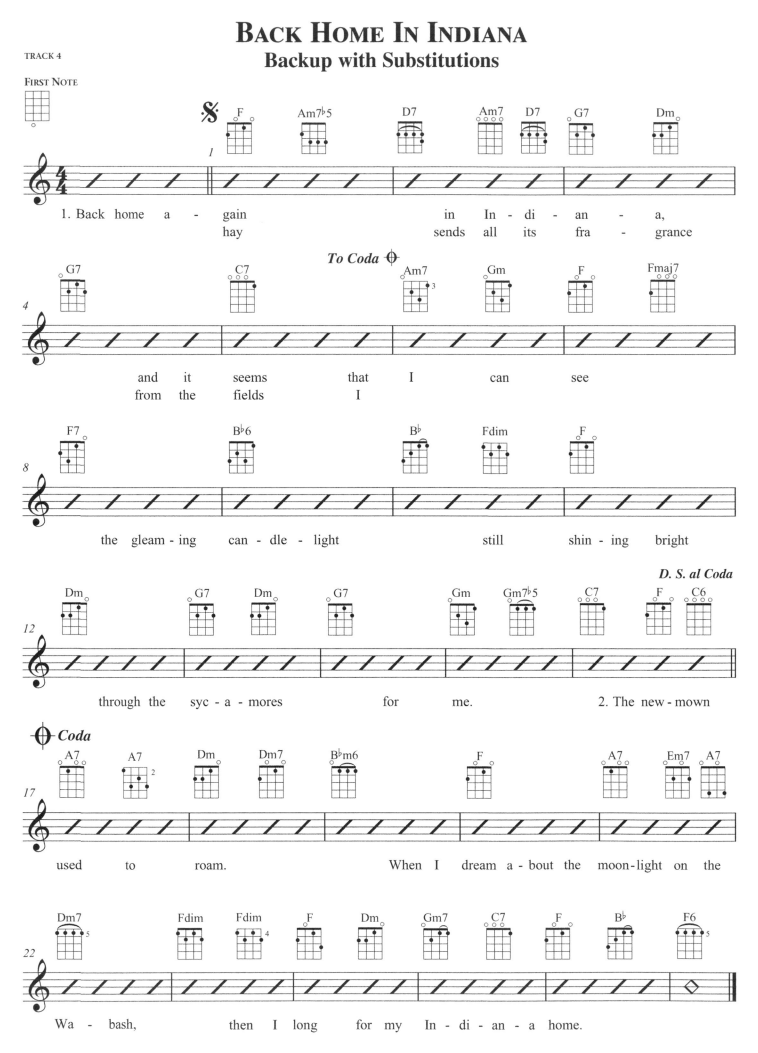

Backup with Substitutions

BACK HOME IN INDIANA
How the Substitutions Work

Bar 1: The Am7♭5 is an example of the *dominant minor substitution* principle:

Dominant Minor Substitution
Given a 7th chord, you can add or substitute the minor chord that is a 5th above it.

The "given 7th chord" in this case is D7, which begins bar 2. Am is a 5th above D7, so it's added into the mix. You can hear how it "sets up" the D7.

Bar 2: The Am7 is another *dominant minor substitution*, just like the Am7♭5 in bar 1. Given an Am chord, any type of Am (such as Am6, Am9, Am7) may sound appropriate. Which brings up another basic substitution principle:

Direct Substitution
You can substitute any chord from the same chord type as the given chord.

For example, given an Am, you could play Am6, Am7, Am7♭5, etc…whichever sounds better to you. Given a C chord you could play any of the major chords: C6, Cmaj7, etc.

Bar 3: Dm is a 5th above the given chord, G7. It's another *dominant minor substitution*.

Bar 6: C7 is the given chord. Am7 is the *relative minor* to C (see the Music Theory chapter on relative minors).

Relative Minor Substitution
You can often substitute a relative minor chord for a major chord.

Given a C, you may be able to play Am instead of, or in addition to the C. Or Am7, or Am6, or any Am chord. Sometimes this idea works for 7th chords as well.

The Gm in bar 6 is the *dominant minor* of C7 (it's a 5th above C7). But what really works in bar 6 is the descending sound you get when you play Am7, Gm, F.

Bar 7: Fmaj7 is a *direct substitution* for F, the given chord. It also creates another descending sound. When you play F, Fmaj7, F7, there's a descending series of notes (F, E, E♭) within the chord sequence. Okay, mark that idea…

Ascending or Descending Melodic Lines
A series of chords can create an ascending or descending melodic line that harmonizes with the song's melody.

This kind of thing tickles the eardrums, because you have two different kinds of melodic movement simultaneously!

Bar 9: B♭6 is a *direct substitution* for B♭.

Bar 10: F diminished is added between the B♭ and the F because it "leads back to" the F, as you can hear when you play the chord sequence: B♭, Fdim, F. Here's the principle that's involved...

Leading Chords
To get from the 4 chord back to the 1 chord, you can often play the 1 diminished (e.g., in the key of F, B♭, Fdim, F).

Also, B♭ and Fdim share two *common notes* (F and D). Sometimes, sharing even one note is a rationale for a substitution (if it sounds good!):

Common Tone Substitution
Sometimes you can substitute a chord that has one or more notes in common with the given chord.

Bar 12: Dm is the *relative minor* of the given chord, F.

Bar 13: The Dm is a *dominant minor substitution* for G7.

Bar 15: Gm and Gm7♭5 are *dominant minor substitutions* for C7. Notice how the Gm – Gm7♭5 – C7 sequence creates a *descending melodic line* on the 3rd string, while the 1st string remains in place. The notes in the melodic line are D, D♭, C, and they harmonize with the song's melody, which is a G note that is sustained over all three chords.

Bar 16: The F chord harmonizes with the song's melody better than C7, and C6 is a *direct substitution* for C7. C6 contains the melody note as well (A).

Bar 18: Dm7 is a *direct substitution* for Dm.

Bar 19: B♭m6 is the 4 minor of F, so it *leads* to the F chord... (B♭m6 is a *direct substitution* of B♭m.)

Leading Chords
The 4 minor often leads back to the 1 chord.

Bar 21: Em7 is a *dominant minor substitution* for A7.

Bar 23: Fdim shares three *common tones* with the given chord, G7. Also G7♭9, a *direct substitution* for G7, is almost the same as Fdim (except for the G note).

Bar 24: Dm is a *relative minor substitution* for F.

Bar 25: Gm7 is a *dominant minor substitution* for C7.

Bar 26: The B♭ is part of a commonly used ending called a ***plagal cadence***...

Plagal Cadence
The 4 chord is often used in the progression at the end of a tune, as part of an ending "amen" flourish, e.g., F B♭ | F instead of two bars of F. Sometimes the 4 chord is followed by the 4 minor, e.g., F B♭ B♭m | F.

Bar 27: F6 is a *direct substitution* for F.

BACK HOME IN INDIANA
Chord/Melody Solo

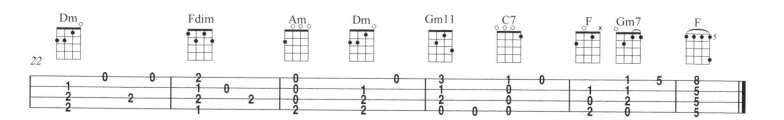

Look For The Silver Lining

Basic Backup and Melody

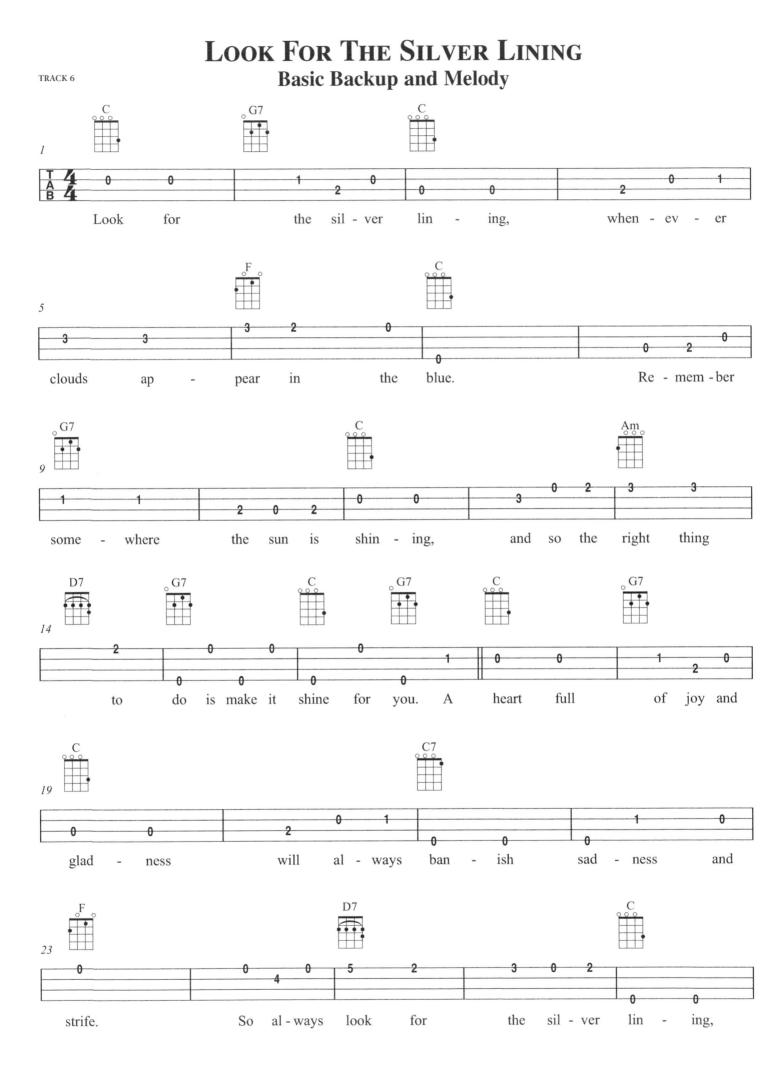

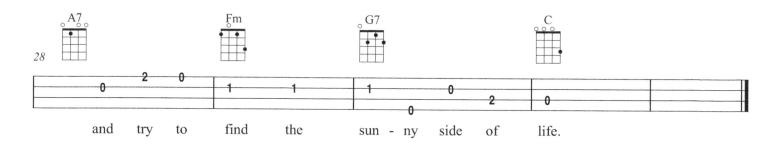

and   try   to   find   the   sun - ny   side   of   life.

LOOK FOR THE SILVER LINING
About the Progression

Many people associate this Jerome Kern/Buddy DeSylva tune with Judy Garland, as she recorded and often performed it. It was written in 1919 for a musical called *Zip, Goes A Million*, and it reappeared the next year in another musical called *Sally*, in which it was sung by Marilyn Miller, a very popular Broadway singer/actress/tap dancer at the time. June Haver played the role of Miller in a 1949 biopic movie musical called *Look For The Silver Lining*, and Judy Garland also portrayed Miller in the 1946 biopic of Kern, *Till The Clouds Roll By*.

Many other famous singers have recorded the tune; Marion Harris's 1920 version was played in the TV show *Downton Abbey*.

Like "Back Home In Indiana," "Look For The Silver Lining" is a 32-bar tune in which the second half (bars 17-32) starts as a repeat of the first half, but has a different ending. Here's the basic progression, in the key of C:

$1 \mid 5^7 \mid 1 \mid 1 \mid 1 \mid 4 \mid 1 \mid 1 \mid 5^7 \mid 5^7 \mid 1 \mid 1 \mid 6\text{-} \mid 2^7 \mid 5^7 \mid 1\ 5^7 \mid$

$1 \mid 5^7 \mid 1 \mid 1 \mid 1^7 \mid 1^7 \mid 4 \mid 4 \mid 2^7 \mid 2^7 \mid 1 \mid 6^7 \mid 4\text{-} \mid 5^7 \mid 1 \mid 1 \parallel$

C | G7 | C | C | C | F | C | C | G7 | G7 | C | C | Am | D7 | G7 | C G7 |

C | G7 | C | C | C7 | C7 | F | F | D7 | D7 | C | A7 | Fm | G7 | C | C ∥

Almost like a folk song, this progression consists mostly of the 1-4-5 chord family, with a relative minor (Am) added into the mix. There are a few other elements:

- The Am, D7, G7, C sequence at the end of the first 16 bars is a 6-, 2, 5, 1 circle-of-fifths phrase.

- The D7 in the second half of the tune is unexpected, but fits the melody.

- The Fm toward the end of the tune is similar to Dm7♭5 (there are three common tones). Therefore, the A7, Fm, G7, C sequence is very similar to a 6, 2, 5, 1.

LOOK FOR THE SILVER LINING
Backup with Substitutions

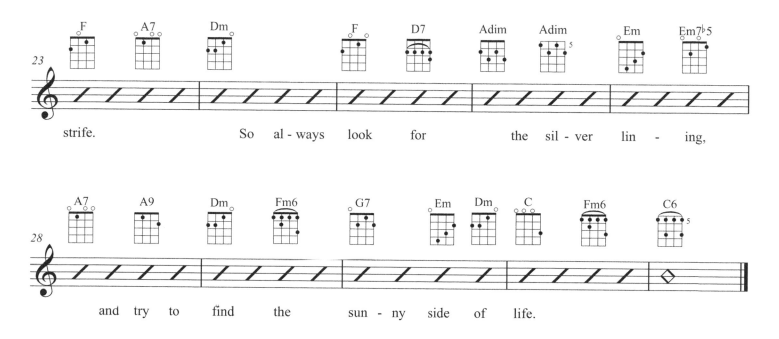

strife. So al - ways look for the sil - ver lin - ing,

and try to find the sun - ny side of life.

LOOK FOR THE SILVER LINING
How the Substitutions Work

Bar 1–2: Am is a *relative minor substitution* for C, and Dm is a *dominant minor substitution* for G7. Together, they turn a simple 1 to 5 change into the "rhythm changes" (1, 6-, 2-, 5).

Bar 3: The F chord creates movement without radically changing anything; it harmonizes with the melody note (C) and you immediately resolve to C.

Bar 4: The G7sus chords *tonicize* the given C chord…

Tonicizing a Chord
Before or after a chord occurs, play its dominant (the chord that is a 5th above it) as a passing chord. This "tonicizes" the given chord; it momentarily makes it a tonic chord and strengthens its position. This works even when the given chord is not the 1 chord (as it is in bar 4); in fact, the chord that is tonicized is usually not the 1 chord.

Bar 6: The Em and Dm create a *diatonic, descending sequence:* F, Em, Dm, C, or 4, 3-, 2-, 1, in the key of C. You go down the scale, from F to C, with diatonic chords, while the melody goes down the scale in harmony with those chords: C, B, A, G.

Diatonic Substitution
Given a bar or two of one chord, a diatonic sequence of chords is played, to create movement. The chord sequence can be ascending or descending, up or down the major scale.

Bar 7: The G7sus *tonicizes* the C chord, as in bar 4.

Bar 8: Am is a *relative minor substitution* for C.

Bar 9: Both Dm chords are *dominant minor substitutions* for G7.

Bar 12: C6 is a *direct substitution* for C.

Bars 13–14: Am(maj7) is a *direct substitution* for Am. Am7 is a *dominant minor substitution* for D7. The three Am chords (Am, Am(maj7), Am7) played in a sequence contain a *descending melodic line* on the fourth string. They are also typical of a ***descending minor chord progression…***

Descending Minor Chord Progression

Given a minor chord, you can substitute a series of minor chords that contain a descending melodic line: minor, minor with a major seventh, minor seventh, minor sixth. For example, instead of Am, play Am, Am(maj7), Am7, Am6. Sometimes the descending melodic line continues and you go to the ♯5 and the 5 of the given chord, like this: Am, Am(maj7), Am7, Am6, Fmaj7, E7. This resembles the "Stairway To Heaven" and "Michelle" progressions.

Bar 15: G7 leads to the C in bar 16, because…

Leading Chords

Dominant 7th chords usually resolve "up a fourth." Seventh chords have tension, and the tension is resolved when you play the chord that is a fourth higher (try it!). For example, G7 leads to C, C7 leads to F, and so on. If, as in this tune, you're playing a G chord and the next chord is C, a G7 "sets up" the C chord.

Bars 17–20 are the same as bars 1–4, and have the same substitutions.

Bar 21: Instead of going directly to C7, the sequence C, Cmaj7, C7 contains a *descending melodic lick* that leads from C to C7. The descending notes are C, B, B♭. The song's melody sustains a G note over all three chords.

Bar 22: Gm7 is a *dominant minor substitution* for C7.

Bars 23 and 24: Dm is a *relative minor substitution* for F. A7 "sets it up," because dominant seventh chords "lead up a fourth."

Bar 25: The F chord delays the D7 by two beats, and is the *relative major* of the Dm in the previous bar.

Relative Major Substitution

Sometimes, given a minor chord, you can substitute its relative major. This is the reverse of *relative minor substitution.*

Bar 26: Adim has three *common tones* (F♯, C and A) with the given chord, D7.

Diminished Chord/Dominant Seventh Substitution

Given a seventh chord, you can substitute a diminished chord that is a 5th higher.

For example, substitute an Adim for D7, or a Gdim for C7.

Here's a related substitution principle…

Diminished Chord Substitution

Given a diminished chord, you can substitute any of the three other diminished chords that share the same notes. Here's why: diminished chords repeat every three frets.

- Play an Adim as shown. (Use the 4th string to name the diminished chords.) It contains these notes: A, E♭, G♭ and C.

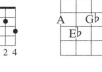

- Now play the same chord 3 frets higher. Notice that it contains the same notes as Adim (C, G♭, A, E♭).

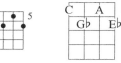

- Another 3 frets higher also contains the same notes: E♭, A, C, G♭.

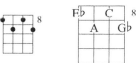

In addition, you could play the same diminished shape three frets higher still at the 11th fret. These four chords are all the same chord, with the same intervals, though the intervals occur in different order. Looking at it another way, every diminished chord has four different names—the names of the four notes that comprise the chord. For example, Adim contains four notes: A, C, E♭ and G♭ (F♯). You can call Adim three other names: Cdim, E♭dim and G♭dim. Therefore, you can substitute Cdim, E♭dim or G♭dim for Adim. That's why there are two diminished chords in bar 26, and both are A diminished.

Bar 27–32: The last five bars of this tune have a 6, 2, 5, 1 progression, if you count the Fm6 as a substitute for Dm7♭5, as mentioned in the "About The Progression" section for this tune. In letters, that's A7, Fm6 (or Dm7♭5), G7, C. The Em and Em7♭5 of bar 27 are "one step back" on the circle-of-fifths, creating a 3, 6, 2, 5, 1 progression.

Here's the general substitution concept…

Extending a Circle-of-Fifths Progression

Given a 1, 6, 2, 5, 1 progression, you can substitute the 3- chord for the first 1 chord. You're "extending the progression" to 3-, 6, 2, 5, 1. This works because the 3- chord shares some notes with the 1 chord; for example, Em is similar to a Cmaj7 chord.

Em7♭5 is a *direct substitution* for Em. Notice how the sequence Em, Em7♭5, A7 includes a descending melodic line (E, D, C♯) on the third string.

Bar 28: A9 is a *direct substitution* for A7.

Bar 29: Dm is the logical 2- to follow the A7, and it harmonizes with the melody, sharing two common tones with Fm. Fm6 is a *direct substitution* for Fm.

Bar 30: Em and Dm harmonize with the melody (E and D notes), and together with the C in bar 31, they create a *diatonic descending chord sequence:* Em, Dm, C.

Bars 31–32: Fm6 is another example of a plagal cadence, a four [4] chord played at the end of a tune to create an ending flourish (1, 4-, 1). C6 is a *direct substitution* for C.

LOOK FOR THE SILVER LINING

Chord/Melody Solo

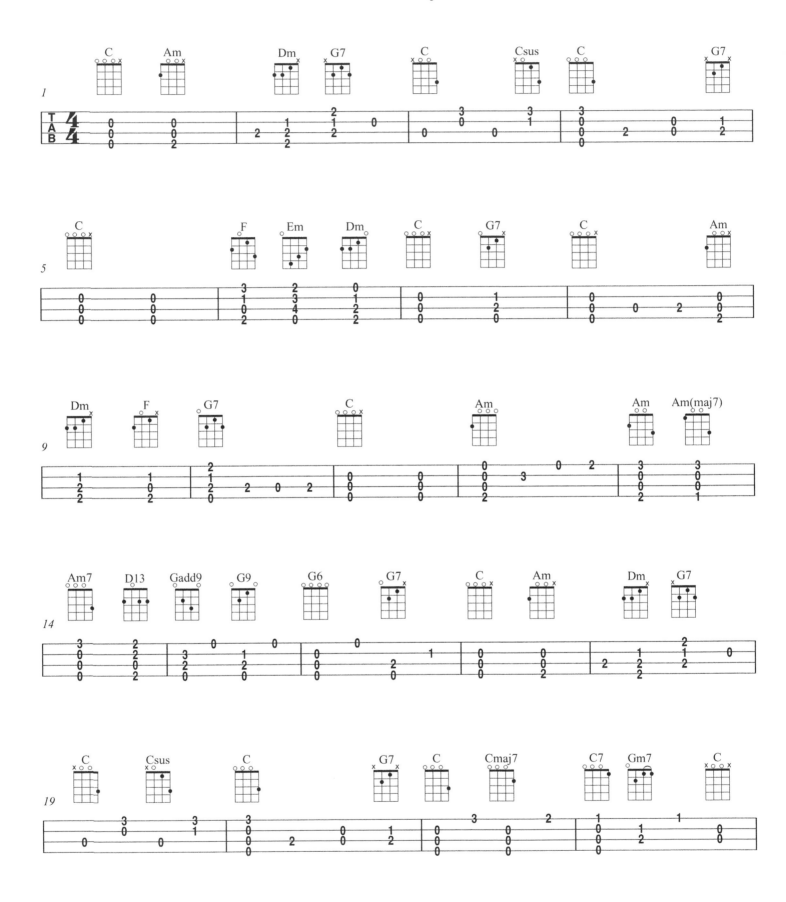

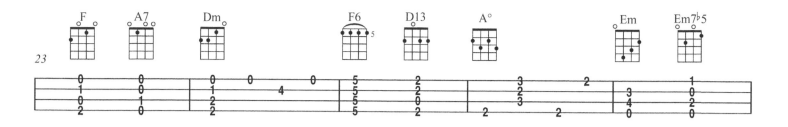

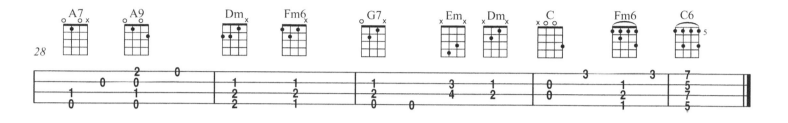

AVALON
Basic Backup and Melody

AVALON
About the Progression

uddy DeSylva ("California, Here I Come," "April Showers," "Button Up Your Overcoat") and
Vincent Rose ("Whispering" and "Blueberry Hill") were among the elite of Tin Pan Alley song-
writers, but a judge ruled that they stole part of "Avalon" from an aria in Puccini's opera, *Tosca* ("E
Lucevan le Stelle"). Nevertheless, their paean to the romantic city on Catalina Island was a huge hit
for Al Jolson in 1921, and he took partial writer's credit for the song, not an unusual thing for star
singers to do in those days. It became a jazz standard and a favorite jamming vehicle for instrumen-
talists like Django Reinhardt, Benny Goodman, Red Nichols and Coleman Hawkins.

Here's the basic progression to this 32-bar tune, in the key of F:

5^7 | 5^7 | 5^7 | 5^7 | 1 | 1 | 1 5^7 | 1 | 1 | 1 | 5^7 | 5^7 | 5^7 | 5^7 | 1 | 1 | 1 5^7 | 1 | 1 | 1 |

6^7 | 6^7 | 6^7 | 6^7 | 2- | 2- 6^7 | 2- | 2- | $1°$ | 1 | 1 | 5 | 6^7 | 6^7 | 2- | 5^7 | 1 | 1 | 1 ‖

C7 | C7 | C7 | C7 | F | F C7 | F | F | C7 | C7 | C7 | C7 | F | F C7 | F | F |

D7 | D7 | D7 | D7 | Gm | Gm D7 | Gm | Gm Fdim | F | F C | D7 | D7 | Gm | C7 | F | F ‖

"Avalon" starts on the 5 chord (C7). This is worth mentioning because many people are under the
false impression that the first chord of a song is the tonic (the 1 chord). In other words, "if it starts on
a C chord, it must be in the key of C"—often, this is not the case. As mentioned in the "Some Basic
Music Theory" chapter of this book, the 1 chord is the chord that *resolves* the progression, the chord
on which you could end the tune. "April Showers" and "Smiles," the next two songs, also start on the
5 chord, and "Some Of These Days" begins on the 3 chord.

The first 16 bars are just the 1 and 5 chords. The second half of the tune starts with a 6, 2, 5, 1, but
the Fdim takes the place of the 5 chord (C7). The song ends with another 6, 2, 5, 1: D7, Gm, C7, F.

AVALON
Backup with Substitutions

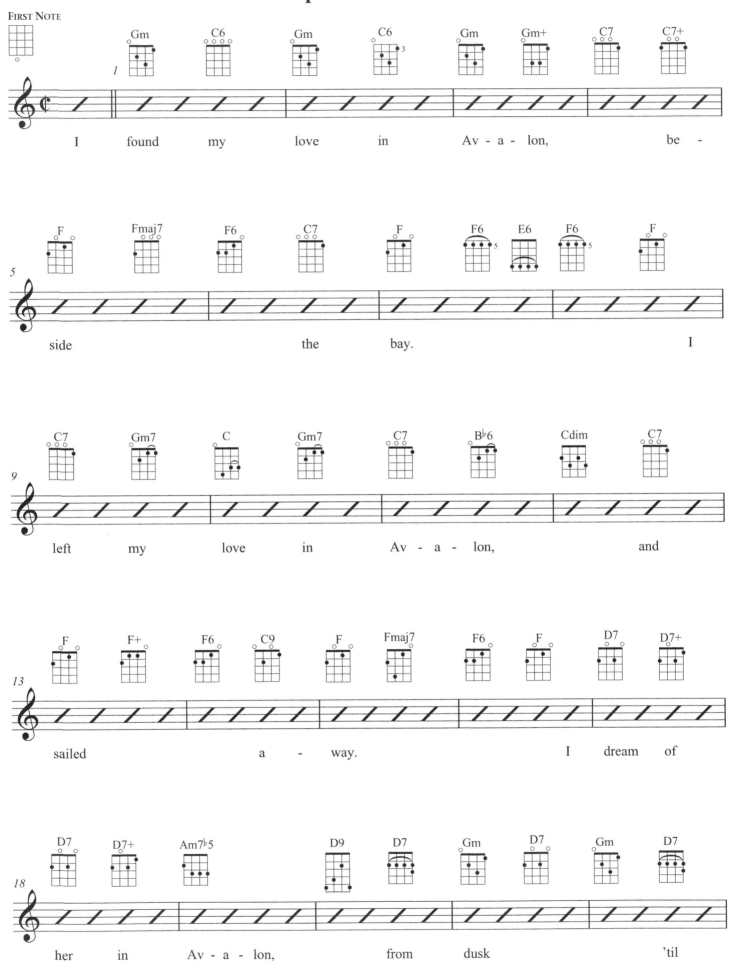

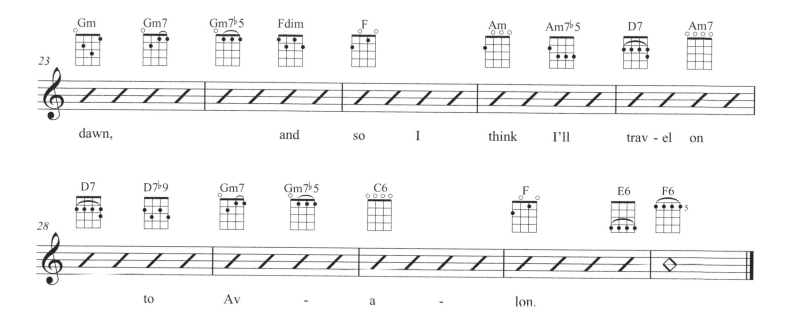

dawn,   and   so   I   think   I'll   trav - el   on

to   Av   -   a   -   lon.

AVALON
How the Substitutions Work

Bars 1–3: Gm and Gm+ are *dominant minor substitutions* for C7. C6 is a *direct substitution* for C7, though they are different types of chords (C6 is a major chord, C7 is a dominant 7th…but they're close enough). The first two bars have an *ascending melodic line* (G, A, B♭, C, on the high strings) that echoes the melody of the song.

Bars 3–4: There's an *ascending melodic line* in the Gm, Gm+, C7 sequence (D, D♯, E). C7+ is a *direct substitute* for C7.

Bars 5–6: Fmaj7 and F6 are *direct substitutions* for F. The sequence of chords in these two bars (F, Fmaj7, F6, C7) contains another *descending line:* F, E, D, C.

Bars 7–8: F6 is a *direct substitution* for F. E6 is a *wiggle chord…*

Wiggle Chords
Sometimes, you move a chord up or down a fret for a beat or two to create movement, even though no chord change is given in the progression. For example, for a bar of C, play C, B, C, C (one beat for each chord).

The up-the-neck F6, E6, F6 sequence creates a nice *fill* where there is a space in the vocal line.

Bars 9–10: Gm7 is a *dominant minor substitution* for C7. There's a chord sequence and melodic *line that ascends and descends* in these two bars. E, F, G, F is the melody line on the second string, and the chord shapes also create the same up and down movement.

Bars 11–12: B♭6 and Cdim are part of a *diatonic fill.* In bars 11–12, instead of two bars of C7, the C7 chord is followed by B♭6, Cdim, C7. Since the uke lacks a low bass note, the diatonic equivalent of that sequence is C7, B♭/D, Cdim, C/E.

Bars 13–15: F+, F6 and Fmaj7 are *direct substitutions* for F, and C9 is a *direct substitution* for C7. This series of chords (F, F+, F6, C9 F) contains an *ascending line* that starts on the 3rd string: C, C♯, D, E, F.

Bars 15–16: Fmaj7 and F6 are *direct substitutions for* F. The series of chords in these two bars contains a *descending melodic line* that starts on the 2nd string in the F chord: F, E, D, C.

Bars 17–18: D7+ is a *direct substitution* for D7. The particular voicings of the chords in these two bars creates an *ascending and descending melodic line* on the 1st string: A, B♭, C, B♭.

Bar 19: Am7♭5 is a *dominant minor substitution* for D7.

Bars 20: D9 is a *direct substitution* for D7. The high D9 chord creates a fill, during a space in the vocal.

Bar 21: D7 *tonicizes* the following Gm.

Bar 23–24: Gm7 and Gm7♭5 are *direct substitutions* for Gm.

Bar 26–30: A 6-, 2, 5, 1, *circle-of-fifths progression* begins at bar 27 (D7, Gm, C7, F). The Am and its direct substitution, Am7♭5, *extend the circle-of-fifths* progression to a 3-, 6, 2-, 5, 1, as in "Look For The Silver Lining," bar 27.

Bar 27: Am7 is a *dominant minor substitution* for D7.

Bar 28: D7♭9 is a *direct substitution* for D7.

Bar 29–30: Gm7 and Gm7♭5 are *direct substitutions* for Gm. Together with the C6 of bar 30, they create a *descending line* on the 3rd string: D, D♭, C. C6 is a *direct substitution* of C7.

Bar 31–32: E6 is an *approach chord*, similar to a *wiggle chord* (see above, bars 7–8)…

Approach Chords
You can anticipate a given chord by one beat, and play the chord that is a fret lower or higher.
For example, the E6 at the end of bar 31 is an *approach chord*; it's followed immediately by the exact same chord a fret higher—F6.

F6, in bar 32, is a *direct substitution* for F.

AVALON

TRACK 11

Chord/Melody Solo

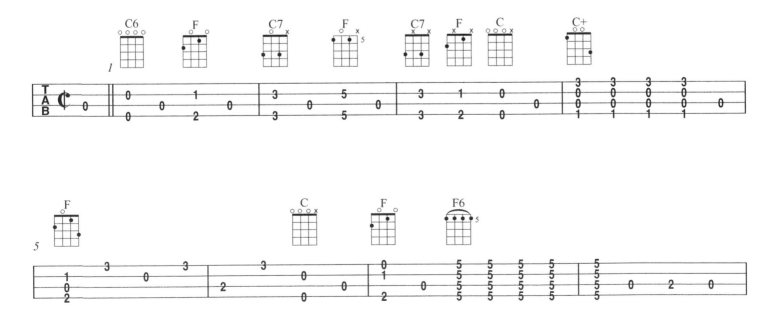

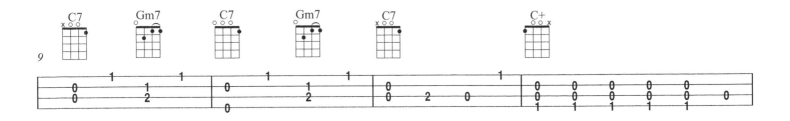

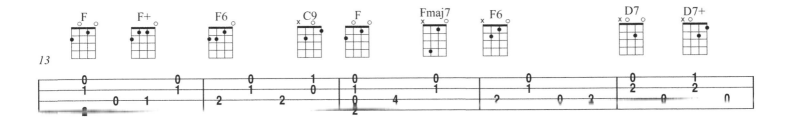

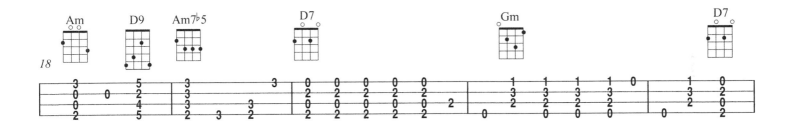

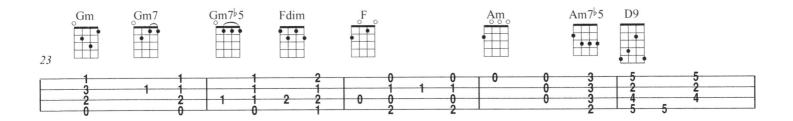

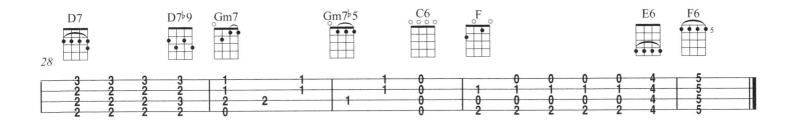

APRIL SHOWERS
Basic Backup and Melody

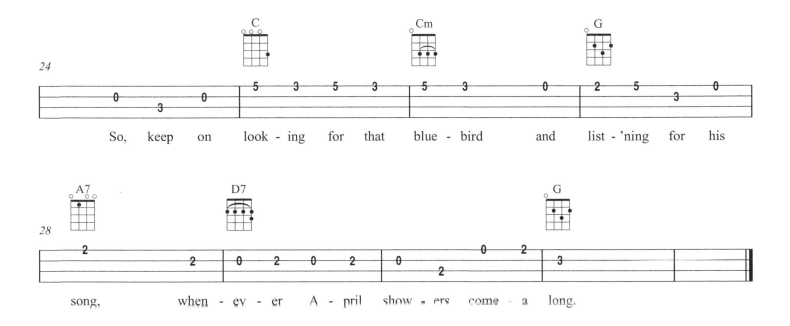

So, keep on look-ing for that blue-bird and list-'ning for his

song, when-ev-er A-pril show-ers come a long.

APRIL SHOWERS
About the Progression

Here's yet another 1921 Al Jolson hit with lyrics written by Bud DeSylva—this time with music by Louis Silvers, whose music appeared in more than 250 movies. Some say the melody is derived from the "Winter" movement of Vivaldi's *Four Seasons*. The song has been recorded by countless crooners, from Bing Crosby and Frank Sinatra to R&B singer Jackie Wilson and The Original Rabbit Foot Spasm Band (an English retro-swing band).

Here's the basic progression, in the key of G. The pickup bar is not included here:

5^7 | 5^7 | 1 | 1 | 1 | 5^7 | 5^7 | 1 | 1 | 1 | 6^7 | 6^7 | 2- | 2- | 2^7 | 2^7 | 5^7 | 5^7 |

5^7 | 5^7 | 1 | 1 | 1 | 6^7 | 6^7 | 2- | 2- | 4 | 4- | 1 | 1 | 2^7 | 5^7 | 5^7 | 1 | 1 | 1 ‖

D7 | D7 | G | G | D7 | D7 | G | G | E7 | E7 | Am | Am | A7 | A7 | D7 | D7 |

D7 | D7 | G | G | E7 | E7 | Am | Am | C | Cm | G | A7 | D7 | D7 | G | G ‖

The first 16 bars begin with a 5, 1, 5, 1 section followed by a circle-of-fifths 6, 2, 5, 1 progression. The next 16 bars start to repeat the first half, but only for 4 bars. Typically, the 4- (Cm) leads back to the 1 chord, and the tune ends with a 2, 5, 1 progression.

APRIL SHOWERS
Backup with Substitutions

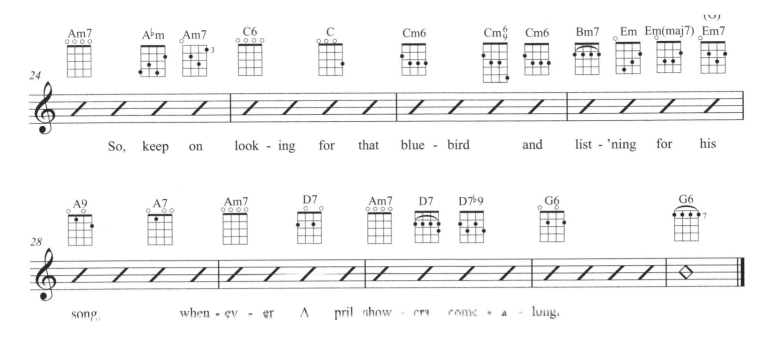

So, keep on look - ing for that blue - bird and list - 'ning for his

song, when - ev - er A - pril show - ers come - a - long.

APRIL SHOWERS
How the Substitutions Work

Pickup Bar: D♭7 is a *wiggle chord,* and it matches the melody note.

Bar 1: Am7 and Am7♭5 are *dominant minor substitutions* for D7.

Bar 2: D♭7 is another *wiggle chord* that goes with the melody.

Bars 3–4: Gmaj7, G6 and G♭5 are *direct substitutions* for G. The sequence G, Gmaj7, G6 contains a *descending melody line* that starts on the 2nd string/3rd fret G note. The G♭5, followed by G mimics the song's melody.

Bar 5: It's the same as bar 1.

Bar 6: D+ is a *direct substitution* for D7. The up-the-neck D+ (at the 5th fret) brings up an *augmented substitution* idea…

Augmented Substitution
Augmented chords repeat every four frets, so you can substitute any of the repeat chords. For example, the augmented shape in bar 6 could also be played at the 9th fret:

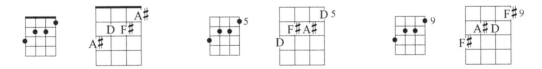

Bars 7–8: G6 and Gmaj7 are *direct substitutions* for G. The D7 is a *tonicizing chord,* but it's followed by Dm, a *dominant substitution* for G. The chord sequence G, D7, Dm, E7 (ending at bar 9) contains a *descending melodic line* that starts with the 2nd string/G note in the G chord: G, F♯, F, E.

Bar 10: Bm7♭5 is a *dominant minor substitution* for E7.

Bar 11: E7♭9 *tonicizes* Am. The chord sequence Am, E7♭9, Am contains a *descending melodic* line on the 1st string: C, B, A.

Bar 12: The three chords in the last three beats of this bar (Am, Am6, Am7) contain an *ascending melodic line* on the 2nd string (E, F♯, G) that mimic the melody.

Bars 13–14: Em, Em(maj7), Em7 and Em6 are *dominant minor substitutions* for A7 and they contain a *descending melodic line* on the 3rd string (E, D♯, D, C♯) that's a counterpoint to the melody. They are typical examples of the *descending minor progression,* as well.

Bar 15: Am and Am7♭5 are *dominant minor substitutions* for D7.

Bars 16–19: Same as the pickup bar and 1–3.

Bar 20: G6 is a *direct substitution* for G, and G♭6 is a *wiggle chord* between the two G6 chords.

Bar 21: Bm7 and Bm7♭5 are *dominant minor substitutions* for E7.

Bar 22: E♭7 is a *wiggle chord* between the two E7 chords.

Bar 23: E7♭9 *tonicizes* Am.

Bar 24: A♭m is another *wiggle chord* between two Am7 chords. Am7 is a *direct substitution* for Am.

Bar 25: C6 is a *direct substitution* for C.

Bar 26: Cm6 and Cm6/9 are *direct substitutions* for Cm.

Bar 27: The last five bars of the song have a 2, 5, 1 *circle-of-fifths progression* (A7, D7, G). The Bm7 and Em chords in bar 27 *extend the circle-of-fifths progression* to a 3-, 6-, 2, 5, 1.

Em(maj7) and Em7 are *direct substitutions* for Em. The three Em chords plus the A9 in bar 28 contain a *descending melodic line* on the 3rd string, and a *descending minor progression,* as in bars 13–14.

Bar 28: A9 is a *direct substitution* for A7.

Bars 29–30: the Am7 chords are *dominant minor substitutions* for D7. D7♭9 is a *direct substitution* for D7.

Bars 31–32: The G6 chords are *direct substitutions* for G. The higher register G6 makes a nice ending chord.

APRIL SHOWERS
Chord/Melody Solo

TRACK 14

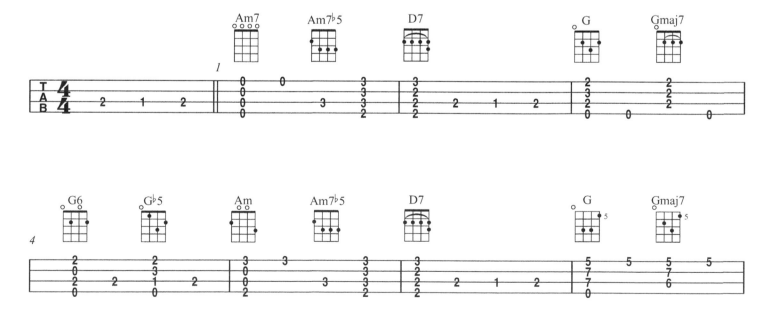

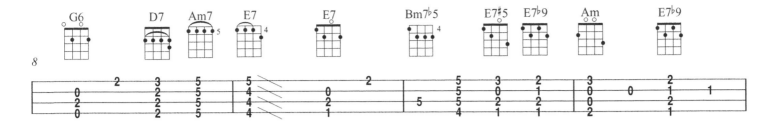

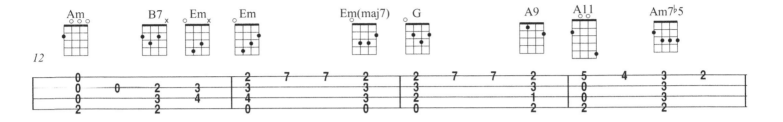

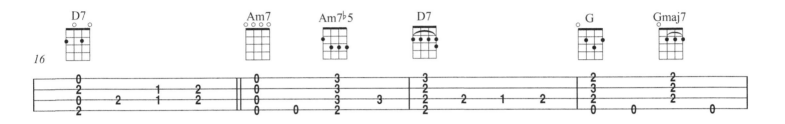

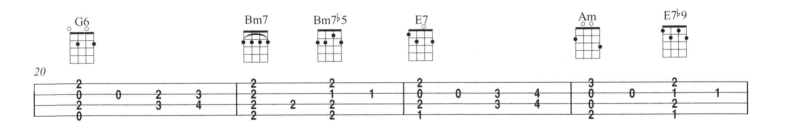

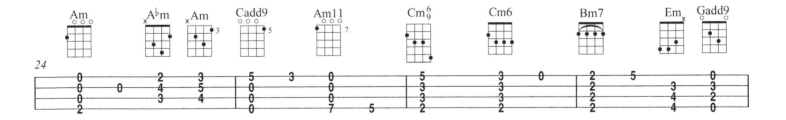

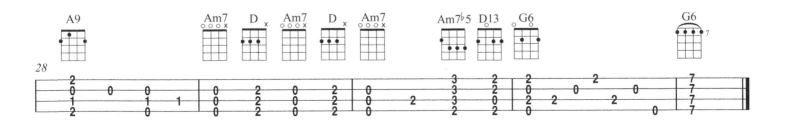

SMILES
Basic Backup and Melody

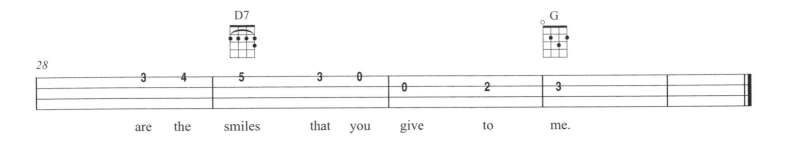

are the smiles that you give to me.

SMILES
About the Progression

In 1917, Lee J. Roberts attended a music business lecture that stressed the business advantages of keeping a smile on your face, and he was inspired to write a song about smiles. His friend, J. Will Callahan wrote the lyrics, and the tune was a smash. The next year it was heard on Broadway in *The Passing Show of 1918*, which also debuted the song "I'm Forever Blowing Bubbles," and featured one of Fred and Adele Astaire's first appearances.

Here's the basic progression, in the key of G:

5^7 | 5^7 | 5^7 | 5^7 | 1 | 1 | 1 | 1 | 3^7 | 3^7 | 6- | 6- | 2^7 | 2^7 | 5^7 | 5^7 |

1^7 | 1^7 | 1^7 | 1^7 | 4 | 4 | 4 | 4 | $1°$ | $1°$ | 1 | 1 | 5^7 | 5^7 | 1 | 1 ‖

D7 | D7 | D7 | D7 | G | G | G | G | B7 | B7 | Em | Em | A7 | A7 | D7 | D7 |

G7 | G7 | G7 | G7 | C | C | C | C | G° | G° | G | G | D7 | D7 | G | G ‖

After eight bars of the 5 chord and 1 chord, "Smiles" has a 3, 6, 2, 5, 1 circle-of-fifths progression. As so often happens, the 1 diminished chord leads you from the 4 chord back to the 1 chord (C, Gdim, G).

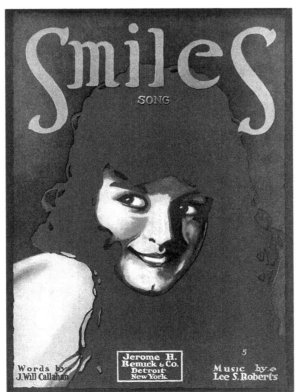

SMILES
Backup with Substitutions

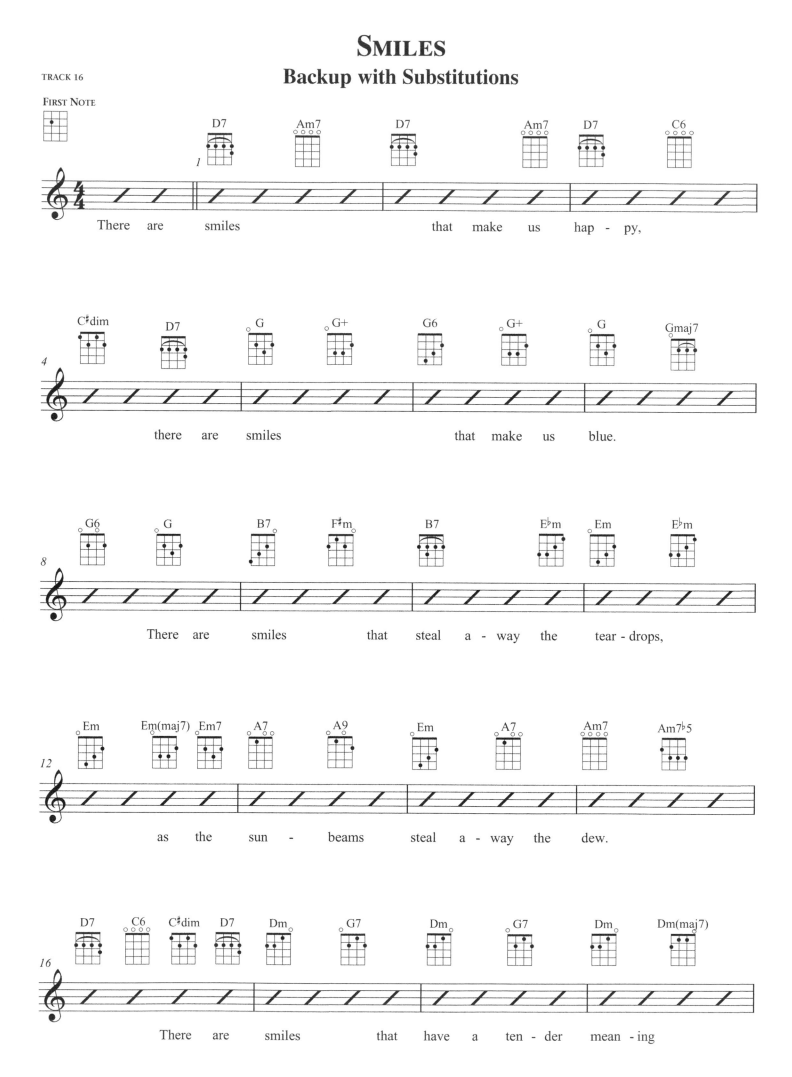

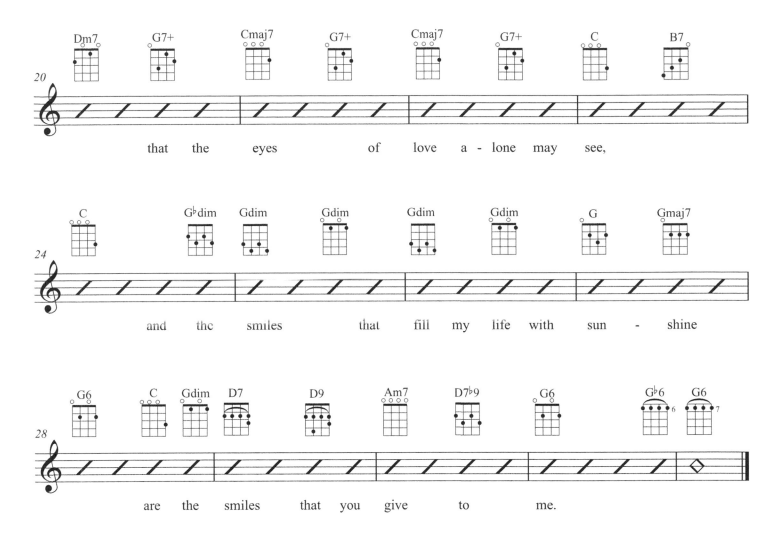

that the eyes of love a - lone may see,

and the smiles that fill my life with sun - shine

are the smiles that you give to me.

SMILES
How the Substitutions Work

Bars 1–2: Am7 is a *dominant minor substitution* for D7.

Bars 3–4: Instead of two bars of D7, a *diatonic* chord sequence is substituted: C6, C♯dim, D7.

Bars 5–6: G+ and G6 are *direct substitutions* for G. There's an *ascending and descending melodic line* within the four chords of these two bars, on the 3rd string: D, D♯, E, D.

Bars 7–8: Gmaj7 and G6 are *direct substitutions* for G. There's a *descending melodic line* (G, F♯, E) on the 2nd string during these bars. It ends on the 3rd string/D note in bar 8.

Bar 9: F♯m is a *dominant minor substitution* for B7.

Bar 10: E♭m is an *approach* chord to Em.

Bar 11: E♭m is a *wiggle chord* between two Em chords.

Bar 12: Em(maj7) and Em7 are *direct substitutions* for Em, and together with the A7 of bar 13, they contain a *descending melodic line* on the 3rd string: E, D♯, D, C♯. They also create a *descending minor progression*.

Bar 13: A9 is a *direct substitution* for A7, and it creates some movement in that bar.

Bar 14: Em is a *dominant minor substitution* for A7.

Bar 15: Am7 and Am7♭5 are *dominant minor substitutions* for D7, and the Am7♭5 also acts as an *approach chord* to D7.

Bar 16: The four chords of this bar create a *diatonic sequence*.

Bars 17–18: The Dm chords in these two bars are *dominant minor substitutions* for G7.

Bars 19–20: The Dm, Dm(maj7) and Dm7 are *dominant minor substitutions* for G7, and they contain a *descending melodic line* on the 3rd string: D, C♯, C. The G7+ is a *direct substitution* for G7. It's a plaintive sounding chord with a lot of tension. Also, notice that this is yet another *descending minor progression* (Dm, Dm(maj7), Dm7).

Bars 21–22: The Cmaj7 chords are *direct substitutions* for C, and the G7+ chords *tonicize* the C chords.

Bar 23: B7 is a *wiggle chord* between two C chords.

Bar 24: G♭dim is an *approach chord* to the Gdim that follows.

Bars 25–26: The different voicings of Gdim create movement while staying on the same chord.

Bars 27–28: Gmaj7 and G6 are *direct substitutions* for G. Together with the G chord they contain a *descending melodic line* on the 2nd string: G, F♯, E. The C and Gdim in bar 28 are *approach chords* to the D7 of bar 29. Together with the destination chord, D7, they create an *ascending melodic line* on the 3rd string: C, D♭, D.

Bar 29: D9 is a *direct substitution* for D7.

Bar 30: Am7 is a *dominant minor substitution* for D7. D7♭9 is a *direct substitution* for D7. It's also an *approach chord* to the G6 in the next bar, as two of its notes drop down a fret when you form the G6 chord.

Bars 31–32: The G6 chords are *direct substitutions* for G, and G♭6 is a *wiggle chord*.

SMILES
Chord/Melody Solo

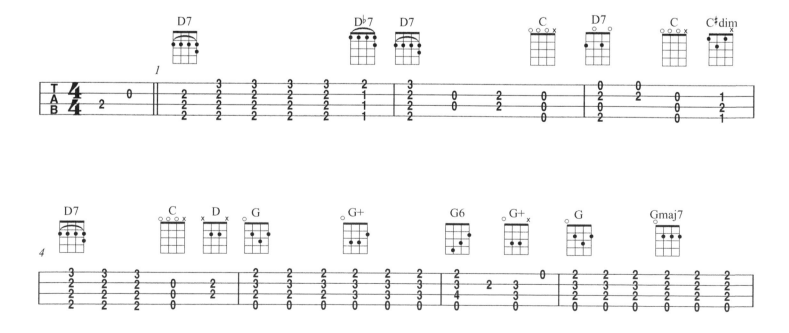

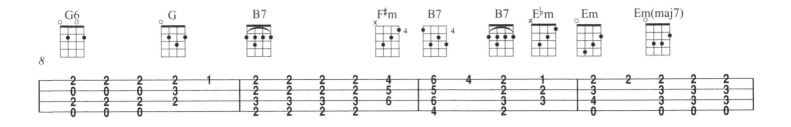

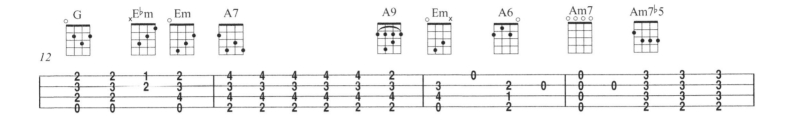

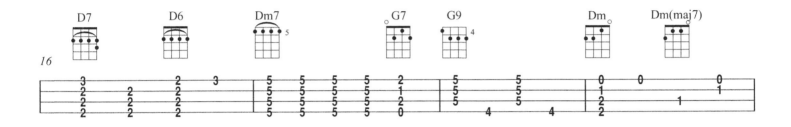

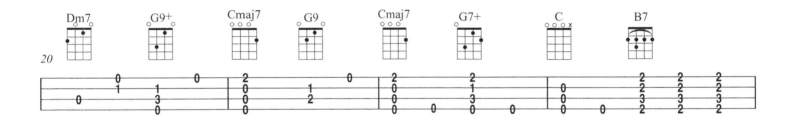

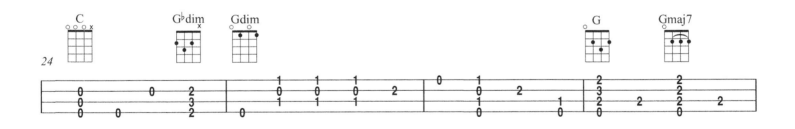

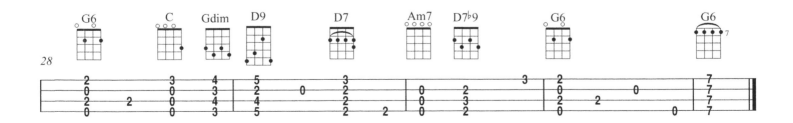

SOME OF THESE DAYS

Basic Backup and Melody

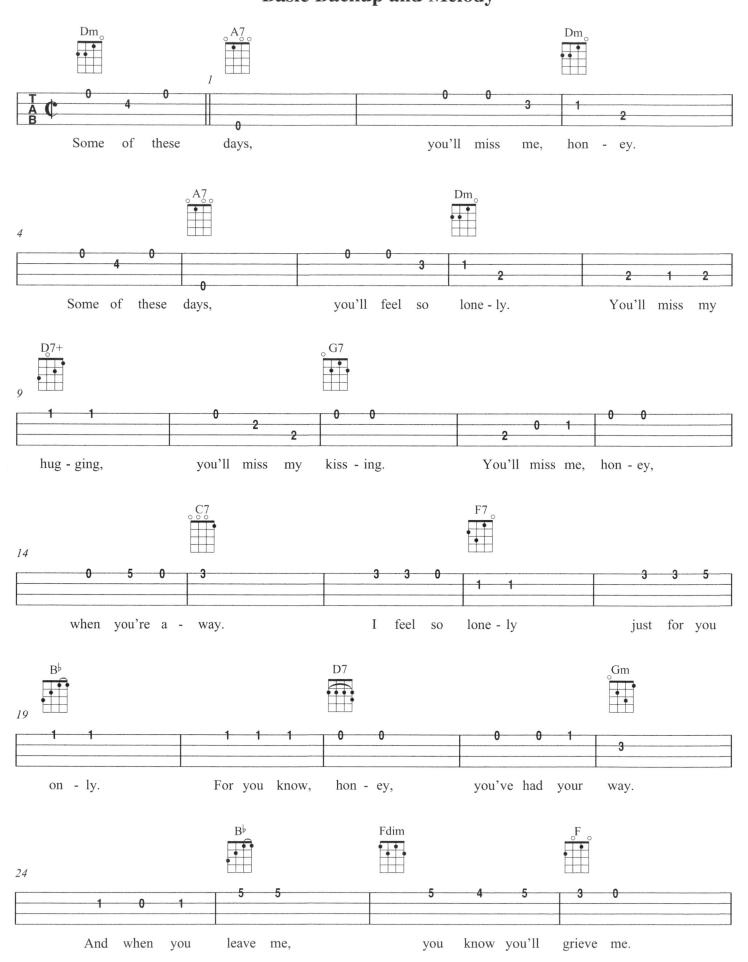

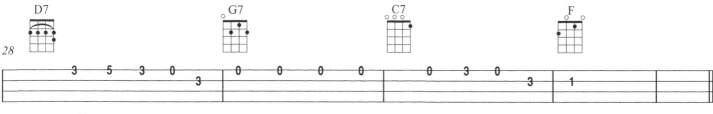

you'll miss your lit - tle   dad - dad - dad - dy,   yes, some of these days.

SOME OF THESE DAYS
About the Progression

Shelton Brooks, who also composed "Darktown Strutters' Ball," hit pay dirt in 1911 when Sophie Tucker not only had a hit with "Some Of These Days," but also made it her theme song for the next half a century. This bluesy showstopper has been used in many movies and was recorded by countless singers, including Louis Armstrong, Judy Garland, Bing Crosby, Brenda Lee, 1920s bluesman Charley Patton, and Cab Calloway. In her autobiography, entitled "Some Of These Days," Tucker said that by 1911 she was already enough of a diva that she was inundated with composers pitching songs, but it was her maid that convinced her to listen to African-American Brooks' tune, and she was glad she did.

Here's the basic progression in the key of F. The pickup bar is not included:

3^7 | 3^7 | 6- | 6- | 3^7 | 3^7 | 6- | 6- | 6^7+ | 6^7+ | 2^7 | 2^7 | 2^7 | 2^7 | 5^7 | 5^7 |

1^7 | 1^7 | 4 | 4 | 6^7 | 6^7 | 2- | 2- | 4 | $1°$ | 1 | 6^7 | 2^7 | 5^7 | 1 | 1 ‖

A7 | A7 | Dm | Dm | A7 | A7 | Dm | Dm | D7+ | D7+ | G7 | G7 | G7 | G7 | C7 | C7 |

F7 | F7 | B♭ | B♭ | D7 | D7 | Gm | Gm | B♭ | F° | F | D7 | G7 | C7 | F | F ‖

Many songs start in a minor key and end in the relative major key. The two keys are identical, because a major chord and its relative minor share the same scale.

For instance, the notes in the Dm scale are the same as in the F major scale. This song starts in Dm and ends in F. If you think of the key as "Dm," A7 is the 5 chord and Gm is the 4 chord. If you consider the key "F," A7 is the 3 chord and Dm is the 6-.

Looking at the key as Dm, the song starts with a couple of 5, 1 phrases. With the D7, you're cycling back on the circle-of-fifths to F, the major key. D7, G7, C7, F is 6, 2, 5, 1. The next D7 sets up the Gm, because it's a 7th chord a fifth above Gm. As usual, F diminished leads back to F, and the tune ends with another 6, 2, 5, 1 progression.

SOME OF THESE DAYS
Backup with Substitution

Some of these days, you'll miss me, hon - ey.

Some of these days, you'll feel so lone - ly.

You'll miss my hug - ging, you'll miss my kiss - ing. You'll miss me,

hon - ey, when you're a - way. I feel so

lone - ly just for you on - ly. For you know,

hon - ey, you've had your way. And when you

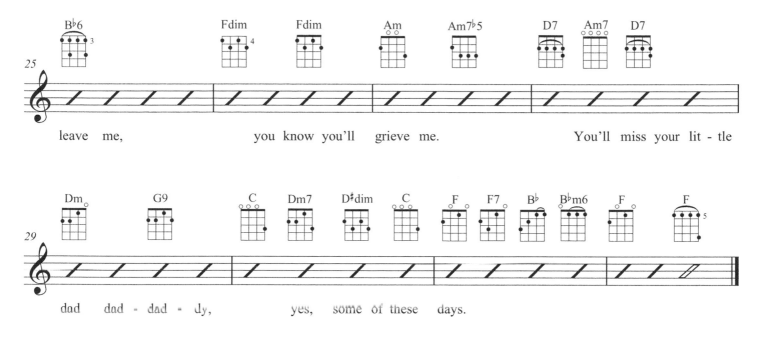

leave me, you know you'll grieve me. You'll miss your lit - tle

dad dad - dad - dy, yes, some of these days.

SOME OF THESE DAYS
How the Substitutions Work

Pickup Bar: D♭m is a *wiggle chord* between the two Dm chords. It matches the song's melody, as well.

Bar 1: Em7♭5 is a *dominant minor substitution* for A7.

Bar 2: A7+ is a *direct substitution* for A7.

Bar 3: A7 *tonicizes* Dm.

Bar 4: same as the pickup bar.

Bar 5: Em is a *dominant minor substitution* for A7, and together with Adim and the A7 in bar 6, it creates a *diatonic ascending series* of chords.

Bar 6: A7+ is a *direct substitution* for A7.

Bars 7–8: In both bars, A7 *tonicizes* Dm.

Bars 9–10: D+, D7 and D9 are all *direct substitutions* for D7+. Using the different chords creates movement.

Bar 11: Dm6 and Dm are *dominant minor substitution*s for G7

Bar 12: Dm is a *dominant minor substitution* for G7, and A7 *tonicizes* Dm. That makes A7 a substitute for a substitute!

Bars 13–14: G9 is a *direct substitution* for G7. Dm, in bar 13, is a *dominant minor substitution* for G7, and together with D♯dim and G7 it creates a *diatonic ascending series* of chords. The Dm in bar 14 is a *dominant minor substitution* for G7.

Bars 15–16: C7, B♭6, Cdim, C is a *diatonic ascending chord sequence*. Bar 16 has a similar sequence (C, B♭add9, C6), minus the diminished chord. C6 is a *direct substitution* for C7. The sixth tone of the C6 chord is the melody note.

Bars 17–18: Cm, Fdim, F7 is another *diatonic ascending chord sequence*. F9 is a *direct substitution* for F7.

Bars 19–20: The B♭6 chords are *direct substitutions* for B♭. A6 is a *wiggle chord* between the two B♭6 chords.

Bars 21–22: C6, C♯dim, D7 create a *diatonic ascending chord sequence*. D7+ is a *direct substitution* for D7, and it matches the song's melody.

Bar 23: D7 *tonicizes* Gm.

Bar 24: B♭ is a *relative major substitution* for Gm. The A chord is a *wiggle chord* between the two Bb chords.

Bar 25: B♭6 is a *direct substitution* for B♭.

Bar 26: Using two different voicings of the Fdim chord creates movement:

Alternate Voicings of a Chord
Playing the same chord several different ways, in different registers, creates movement. For example, given two bars of G, you can alternate between two different G chords (in two registers), playing two beats per chord voicing.

Bar 27: The last five bars of the tune (bars 28–32) are a 6, 2, 5, 1 *circle-of-fifths progression* (D7, G7, C7, F). The Am in bar 27 *extends the circle-of-fifths progression* (since Am is one step back on the circle) to a 3-, 6, 2, 5, 1 progression. Am7♭5 is a *direct substitution* for Am.

Bar 28: Am7 is a *dominant minor substitution* for D7.

Bar 29: Dm is a *dominant minor substitution* for G7. G9 is a *direct substitution* for G7.

Bars 30–31: C is a *direct substitution* for C7, and C, Dm7, D♯dim, C, F is yet another *diatonic ascending chord sequence*. It contains an *ascending melodic line* that starts on the 3rd string: C, D, D♯, E, F.

Bar 31: The F7, B♭, B♭m6, F sequence is a typical *blues turnaround* used to end a blues verse or a bluesy song…

Blues Turnaround
At the end of a bluesy song, or a verse, instead of two bars of the 1 chord, play: 1 17 4 4- | 1 |

Bar 32: It's effective to end a tune with a high-register chord, like the second F chord in this bar.

Some Of These Days
Chord/Melody Solo

TRACK 20

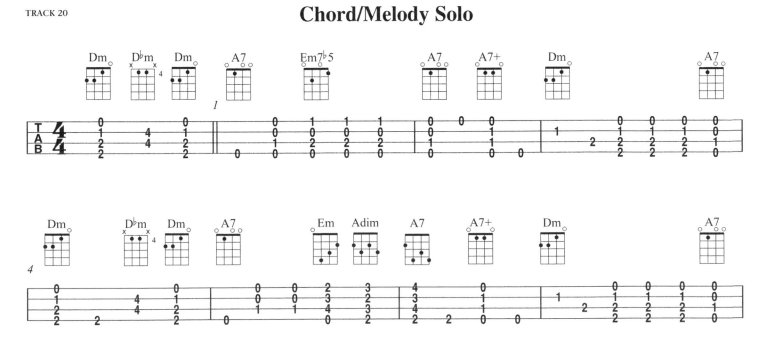

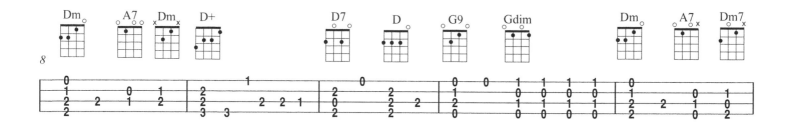

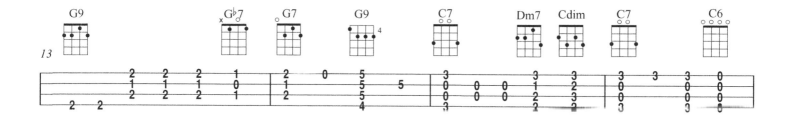

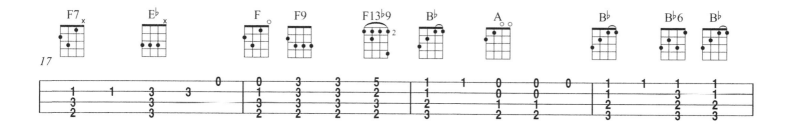

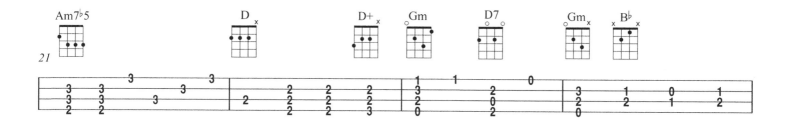

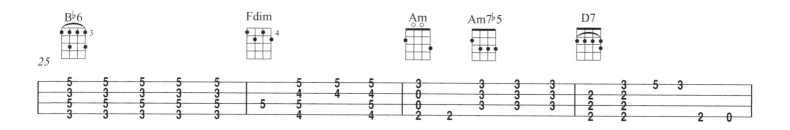

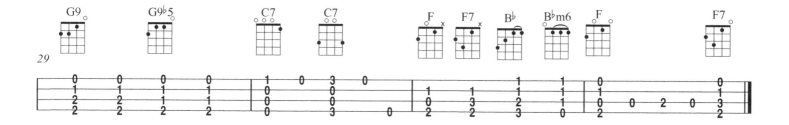

I'm Always Chasing Rainbows
Basic Backup and Melody

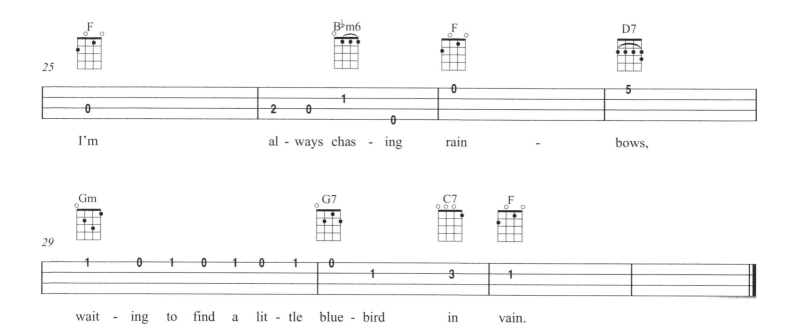

I'm Always Chasing Rainbows
About the Progression

I'm Always Chasing Rainbows" was published in 1917, with lyrics by Joseph McCarthy (no, not *that* Joseph McCarthy of the 1950s!), who was already famous for "You Made Me Love You" and would soon write "Alice Blue Gown." The composer was Harry Carroll, who had also written "By The Beautiful Sea" three years earlier. He borrowed the first dozen bars of "Rainbows" from the mid-section of Chopin's *Fantaisie-Impromptu, Op. 66*.

Introduced by the very popular Dolly Sisters in Broadway's *Oh, Look!*, the song was first recorded in 1918 by vaudeville dancer/comedian Harry Fox, after whom the Fox Trot was named. Used in numerous movies, it has been a hit many times over, and the impressive list of singers who have recorded it (in every decade since it appeared) ranges from Al Jolson to Alice Cooper.

Here's the basic progression, in the key of F:

$1 \mid 1 \; 4\text{-} \mid 1 \mid 1 \mid 5^7 \mid 5^7 \; 1 \mid 5^7 \mid 5^7 \mid 6^7 \mid 6^7 \mid 2\text{-} \; 6^7 \mid 2\text{-} \mid 2^7 \mid 2^7 \mid 5^7 \mid 5^7 \mid$

$1^7 \mid 1^7 \mid 4 \mid 4 \mid 6^7 \mid 6^7 \mid 2^7 \mid 5^7 \mid 1 \mid 1 \; 4\text{-} \mid 1 \mid 6^7 \mid 2\text{-} \mid 2^7 \; 5^7 \mid 1 \mid 1 \parallel$

F | F B♭m | F | F | C7 | C7 F | C7 | C7 | D7 | D7 | Gm D7 | Gm | G7 | G7 | C7 | C7 |

F7 | F7 | B♭ | B♭ | D7 | D7 | G7 | C7 | F | F B♭m | F | D7 | Gm | G7 C7 | F | F ‖

There's a 6, 2, 5, 1 circle-of-fifths progression in the middle of the 32 bars: D7, Gm, G7, C7, F. Two more 6, 2, 5, 1 sequences happen in the second half of the song as well.

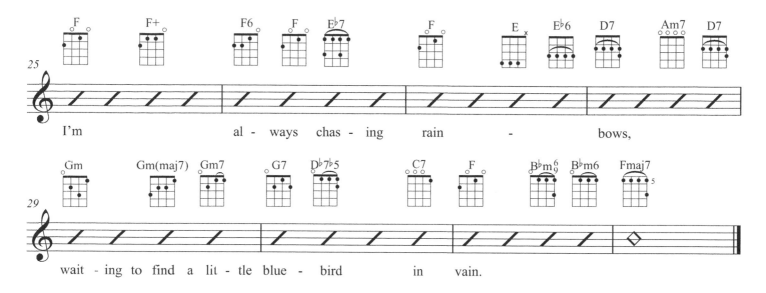

I'm   al - ways   chas - ing   rain -   bows,

wait - ing to find a lit - tle blue - bird   in   vain.

I'M ALWAYS CHASING RAINBOWS
How the Substitutions Work

Bars 1–2: Fmaj7 and F6 are *direct substitutions* for F. The four F chords that begin the tune contain a *descending melodic line* that begins on the 2nd string/F note: F, E, D, C. B♭m6 is a *direct substitution* for B♭m.

Bars 3–4: The F chords are the same as in bars 1-2 and have the same *descending melodic line.*

Bars 5–6: Gm7 and Gm are *dominant minor substitutions* for C7. The four chords of these bars contain a *descending melodic line*: B♭, A, G, F. C6 is a *direct substitution* for C7.

Bars 7–8: The four chords of these two bars create a *diatonic ascending chord sequence.* It contains an *ascending melodic line*, starting on the 3rd string of the C7 chord: C, D, E♭, E.

Bars 9–10: Am7 and Am7♭5 are *dominant minor substitutions* for D7. The chords of bar 10 contain the song's melody line.

Bar 11: D7♭9 is a *direct substitution* for D7. It lends a more melancholy tone than D7.

Bar 12: Gm(maj7) and Gm7 are *direct substitutions* for Gm. The three chords of this bar contain a *descending melodic line* that starts on the 3rd string of the Gm chord: G, F♯, F.

Bars 13–14: Dm and Dm(maj7) are *dominant minor substitutions* for G7. The two chords of bar 14, together with the C7 of bar 15, contain a *descending melodic line* that starts on the 3rd string of Dm: D, C♯, C.

Bars 15–16: This is the same *diatonic ascending chord sequence* as in bars 7–8.

Bars 17–18: The three Cm chords are *dominant minor substitutions* for F7, and F7♭9 is a *direct substitution* for F7. The four chords of these two bars, plus the B♭ chord that begins bar 19, contain a *descending melodic line* that begins on the 4th string: B♭, A, G, F♯, F.

Bar 19: F7♭9 *tonicizes* B♭.

Bar 20: B♭6 is a *direct substitution* for B♭. The three *alternate voicings* of B♭ create a feeling of movement.

Bars 21–22: The Am7♭5 chords are *dominant minor substitutions* for D7. Cm7 is a *common tone substitution* for Am7♭5 (a substitution for a substitution). It only differs from Am7♭5 by one note, and the different note happens to be the melody note of the tune.

Bar 23: D♭7♭5 is a *flat five substitution* for G7...

Flat Five Substitution

Often, you can play a seventh chord that is a flatted fifth above a given chord. This works well especially in circle-of-fifths progressions. For example, instead of this 2-, 5, 1 progression in C—Dm, G7, C; play Dm, D♭7, C (the D♭7 is a *flat five substitution* for G7, as D♭ is a flatted fifth above G).

Bar 24: C9 and C7♭9 are *direct substitutions* for C7. The three chords of this bar, plus the first chord of bar 25, contain a *descending melodic line* that starts on the 2nd string of the C7 chord: E, D, D♭, C.

Bars 25–26: F+ and F6 are *direct substitutions* for F. The sequence F, F+, F6 has an *ascending melodic line* that starts on the 3rd string of the F chord—C, C♯, D. E♭7 is a *reverse dominant minor substitution* for B♭m...

Reverse Dominant Minor Substitution

This is the opposite of dominant minor substitution. Sometimes, given a minor chord, you can play the 7th chord that is a fourth above it. For example: instead of B♭m, play E♭7, a fourth higher. (In dominant minor substitution, you would substitute B♭m for E♭7.)

Bar 27: E and E♭6 are part of a *descending 1 to 6 progression*...

Descending from 1 to 6

When going from the 1 chord to the 6 chord at the beginning of a 6, 2, 5, 1 (circle-of-fifths) progression, you can "walk down" the chords from 1 to 6, like this: instead of C | A7 | D7 G7 | D ‖ play: C B B♭ | A7 | D7 G7 | C ‖

Bar 28: Am7 is a *dominant minor substitution* for D7.

Bar 29: Gm(maj7) and Gm7 are *direct substitutions* for Gm. The three Gm chords of this bar contain a *descending melodic line* on the 2nd string: G, F♯, F. They also create a *descending minor progression*.

Bar 30: D♭7♭5 is a *flat five substitution* for G7. Typically, it's part of a circle-of-fifths, 6, 2, 5, 1 progression.

Bars 31–32: B♭m6/9 and B♭m6 (leading to the final 1 chord) are a variation of a *plagal cadence*. Fmaj7 is a *direct substitution* for F.

I'M ALWAYS CHASING RAINBOWS

TRACK 23

Chord/Melody Solo

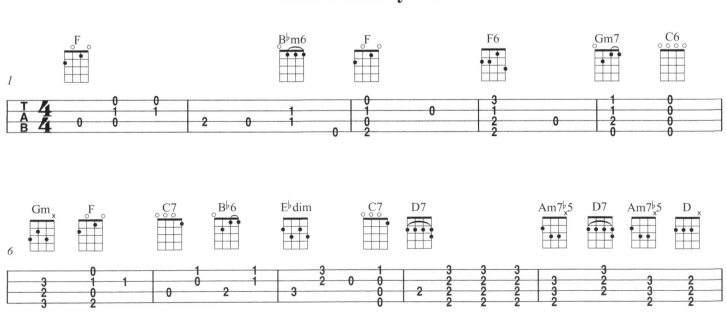

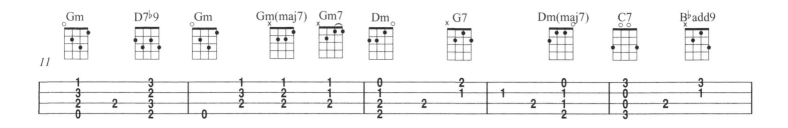

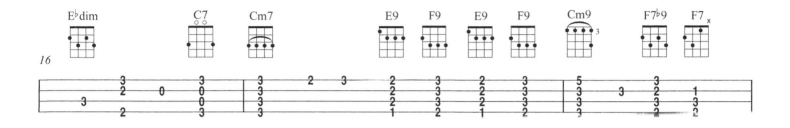

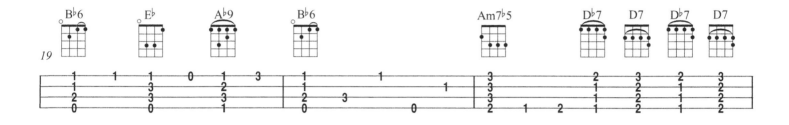

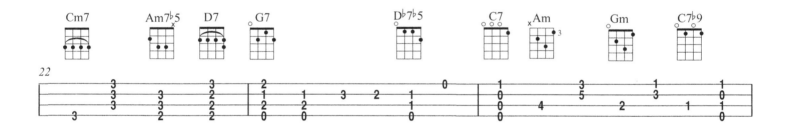

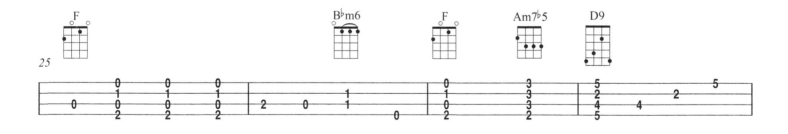

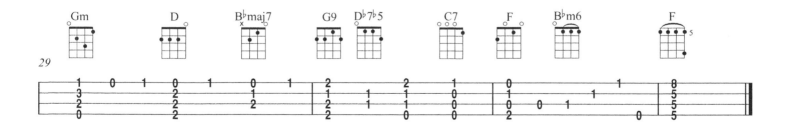

Index Of Substitution Principles

Here are all the substitution ideas mentioned in this book, in alphabetical order, with a notation on the first time they occurred in the text. **All bar numbers refer to the backup with substitution arrangements.**

Alternate Voicings of a Chord
Playing the same chord several different ways, in different registers, creates movement. For example, given two bars of G, alternate between two different G chords (in two registers), playing two beats per chord voicing. See "Some Of These Days," bar 26.

Approach Chords
You can anticipate a given chord by one beat, and play the chord that is a fret lower or higher. For example, a bar of E can be played: E♭6, E6, E6, E6. See "Avalon," bars 31–32.

Ascending or Descending Melodic Lines
A series of chords can create an ascending or descending melodic line that harmonizes with the song's melody. This kind of thing tickles the eardrums, because you have two different kinds of melodic movement simultaneously! See "Back Home In Indiana," bar 7.

Augmented Substitution
Augmented chords repeat every four frets, so you can substitute any of the repeat chords. See "April Showers," bar 6.

Blues Turnaround
At the end of a bluesy song, or a verse, instead of two bars of the 1 chord, play: 1 17 4 4- | 1 |
See "Some Of These Days," bar 31.

Common Tone Substitution
Sometimes you can substitute a chord that has one or more notes in common with the given chord. See "Back Home In Indiana," bar 10.

Descending from 1 to 6
When going from the 1 chord to the 6 chord at the beginning of a 6, 2, 5, 1 (circle-of-fifths) progression, you can "walk down" the chords from 1 to 6, like this: instead of C | A7 D7 G7 | C ‖ play: C B B♭ | A7 | D7 G7 | C ‖ See "I'm Always Chasing Rainbows," bar 27.

Descending Minor Chord Progression
Given a minor chord, you can substitute a series of minor chords that contain a descending melodic line—minor, minor with a major seventh, minor seventh, minor sixth. For example, instead of Am, play Am, Am(maj7), Am7, Am6. Sometimes the descending melodic line continues and you go to the ♯5 and the 5 of the given chord, like this: Am, Am(maj7), Am7, Am6, Fmaj7, E7. This resembles the "Stairway To Heaven" and "Michelle" progressions. See "Look For The Silver Lining," bars 13–14.

Diatonic Substitution
Given a bar or two of one chord, a diatonic sequence of chords is played, to create movement. The chord sequence can be ascending or descending, up or down the major scale. See "Look For The Silver Lining," bar 6.

Diminished Chord/Dominant Seventh Substitution
Given a seventh chord, you can substitute a diminished chord that is a 5th higher. For example, substitute an Adim for D7, or a Gdim for C7. See "Look For The Silver Lining," bar 26.

Diminished Chord Substitution
Given a diminished chord, you can substitute any of the three other diminished chords that share the same notes. Here's why: Diminished chords repeat every three frets. See "Look For The Silver Lining," bar 26.

Direct Substitution

You can substitute any chord from the same chord type as the given chord. See "Back Home In Indiana," bar 2.

Dominant Minor Substitution

Given a 7th chord, you can add or substitute the minor chord that is a 5th above it. See "Back Home In Indiana," bar 1.

Extending a Circle-of-Fifths Progression

Given a 1, 6, 2, 5, 1 progression, you can substitute the 3- chord for the first 1 chord. You're "extending the progression" to 3-, 6, 2, 5, 1. This works because the 3- chord shares some notes with the 1 chord; for example, Em is similar to a Cmaj7 chord. Also, you're going back one step further on the circle-of-fifths (the 3 chord is a fifth above the 6 chord). See "Look For The Silver Lining," bar 27.

Flat Five Substitution

Often, you can play a seventh chord that is a flatted fifth above a given chord. This works especially in circle-of-fifths progressions. For example, instead of this 2-, 5, 1 progression in C—Dm, G7, C; play Dm, Db7, C. The Db7 is a flat five substitution for G7, as Db is a flatted fifth above G. See "I'm Always Chasing Rainbows" bar 23.

Leading Chords

Dominant 7th chords usually resolve "up a fourth." Seventh chords have tension, and the tension is resolved when you play the chord that is a fourth higher. See "Look For The Silver Lining," bar 15.

Leading Chords

The 4 minor often leads back to the 1 chord. See "Back Home In Indiana," bar 19.

Leading Chords

To get from the 4 chord back to the 1 chord, you can often play the 1 diminished (e.g., in the key of F: Bb, Fdim, F). See "Back Home In Indiana," bar 10.

Plagal Cadence

The 4 chord is often used at the end of a tune, as part of an ending "amen" flourish, e.g., F Bb | F instead of two bars of F. Sometimes the 4 chord is followed by the 4 minor, e.g., F Bb Bbm | F. See "Back Home In Indiana," bar 26.

Relative Major Substitution

Sometimes, given a minor chord, you can substitute its relative major. This is the reverse of the more common *relative minor substitution* below. See "Look For The Silver Lining," bar 25.

Relative Minor Substitution

Often, you can substitute a relative minor chord for a major chord. See "Back Home In Indiana," bar 6.

Reverse Dominant Minor Substitution

This is the opposite of dominant minor substitution. Sometimes, given a minor chord, you can play the 7th chord that is a fourth above it. For example: instead of Bbm, play Eb7, a fourth higher. (In *dominant minor substitution*, you would substitute Bbm for Eb7.) See "I'm Always Chasing Rainbows," bar 26.

Tonicizing a Chord

Before or after a chord occurs, play its dominant (the chord that is a 5th above it) as a passing chord. This "tonicizes" the given chord; it momentarily makes it a tonic chord and strengthens its position. See "Look For The Silver Lining," bar 4.

Wiggle Chords

Sometimes, you move a chord up or down a fret for a beat or two to create movement, even though no chord change is given in the progression. For example, for a bar of C, play C, B, C, C (one beat for each chord). See "Avalon," bars 7–8.

About The Author

Fred Sokolow is best known as the author of over a hundred and fifty instructional and transcription books and DVDs for guitar, banjo, Dobro, mandolin, lap steel and ukulele. Fred has long been a well-known West Coast, multi-string performer and recording artist, particularly on the acoustic music scene. The diverse musical genres covered in his books and DVDs, along with several bluegrass, jazz and rock CDs he has released, demonstrate his mastery of many musical styles. Whether he's playing Delta bottleneck blues, bluegrass or old-time banjo, 'thirties swing guitar, Hawaiian uke or screaming rock solos, he does it with authenticity and passion.

Fred's other ukulele books include:

- *Fretboard Roadmaps for Ukulele*, book/audio (with Jim Beloff), Hal Leonard Corporation

- *Blues Ukulele*, book/audio, Flea Market Music, distributed by Hal Leonard Corporation

- *Bluegrass Ukulele*, book/audio, Flea Market Music, distributed by Hal Leonard Corporation

- *101 Ukulele Tips*, book/audio, Hal Leonard Corporation

- *Fingerstyle Ukulele*, book/audio, Hal Leonard Corporation

- *Beatles Fingerstyle Ukulele*, Hal Leonard Corporation

Email Fred with any questions about this or his other ukulele books at: *sokolowmusic.com*